"LEE'S DEFINITIONS ARE CLEAR, EASY-TO-UNDERSTAND, AND OFTEN WRITTEN WITH A WITTY EDGE. ... EXCELLENT ... FOR INNOCENTS AND EVEN EXPERTS."
—*Dayton News*

"FOR YEARS, I'VE ENJOYED EVERY WORD SUSAN LEE HAS WRITTEN ABOUT ECONOMICS AND FINANCE. ..."
—Peter Martin, Editorial Director, The Economist Publications

"IF YOU ARE IMPATIENT WITH LONG-WINDED EXPLANATIONS AND NEED TO KNOW ABOUT THINGS ECONOMIC AND FINANCIAL ... SUSAN LEE'S BOOKS CAN GIVE YOU A JUMP ON KEY IDEAS."
—*Wilmington News*

"SUBSTANTIAL INFORMATION TO HELP A NOVICE UNDERSTAND WALL STREET ... REFRESHING."
—*The New York Times Book Review*

"[A] WEALTH OF INFORMATION ... ADMIRABLE CONCISION AND A STYLE THAT NEVER LEANS TOWARD THE CONDESCENDING. ... LEE OBVIOUSLY KNOWS HER BUSINESS."
—*USA Today*

Books by Susan Lee

Susan Lee's ABZs of Economics
Susan Lee's ABZs of Money and Finance

Published by POCKET BOOKS

SUSAN LEE'S

ABZs
of MONEY & FINANCE

POCKET BOOKS

New York   London   Toronto   Sydney   Tokyo

POCKET BOOKS, a division of Simon & Schuster Inc.,
1230 Avenue of the Americas, New York, N.Y. 10020

Published by arrangement with the author

ISBN: 0-671-67440-4

First Pocket Books trade paperback printing July 1989

10 9 8 7 6 5 4 3 2 1

POCKET and colophon are trademarks
of Simon & Schuster Inc.

Printed in the U.S.A.

Acknowledgments

Very many thanks to those who ploughed through the manuscript: Christie Brown, Bill Baldwin, Peter Brimelow, Maggy Laws, and Ken Weisshaar. Many thanks to my agent, Ginger Barber, and my editor, Elaine Pfefferblit; and to those who provided technical help, Frank Lijoi and Tim Hailand. Thanks to those who kept me cheerful and working: Susan Chace, Bob Wilson, Peter Martin, Nick Von Hoffman, Jon Previant, and Commando Hubbell. And special thanks to the people who turned me loose on the financial markets in the first place, Jim Michaels and Bob Bartley.

To Big Pidge, Ken-Bob and Spenny.

List of Entries

Acquisition
ADR
Affiliated Company
American Stock Exchange
Amortize, Amortization
Annual Report
Annuity
Appreciation (Assets)
Appreciation (Currency)
Arbitrage
Asset

Balance Sheet
Balloon Payment
Bank Failure
Bankruptcy
Banks and Banking
Barter
Basis Point
Bath (or, often, Big Bath)
Bear
Beta Coefficient
Block Trade
Blue Chip
Bond
Bond Yield
Book Value

Broker
Bull
Business Cycle
Buyer's Market

Call
Callable
Capital
Capital Gain (or Loss)
Capital Market
Capitalized Value,
    Capitalization Rate
Cash
Cash Flow
Certificate of Deposit
Churning
Closed-End Mutual Fund or
    Closed-End Investment
    Company
Closely Held Corporation or
    Closed Corporation
Commercial Paper
Commission
Commodity
Common Stock
Conglomerate
Consumer Price Index

Partnership
Par Value
Pension Fund
Ponzi Scheme
Portfolio
Preferred Stock
Price-Earnings Ratio
Prime Rate
Profits
Pro Forma
Program Trading
Proprietorship
Proxy
Put

Quotation

Random Walk Hypothesis
Real Estate Investment Trust
Registration Statement
Revenue Bond
Risk
Rollover

Savings
Securities
Securities and Exchange
    Commission
Short
Sinking Fund
Speculation

Spot Market
Spread
Standard & Poor's 500
    Composite Index
Stock Dividend, Stock Split
Stock Exchange
Stop Order

Takeover
Taxes
Tax-Exempt
Tender Offer
Tight Money
Treasury Securities
Treasury Stock
Trust

Underwriting
Unlisted Security

Variable Rate
Venture Capital

Wall Street
Warrant

Yield
Yield Curve

Zero Coupon Bond

Introduction

Generally speaking, an introduction should offer an outline of the book, a taste of how stylishly the author writes, a promise of specific enlightenment, and an exhortation to keep turning the pages—all delivered in a suitably upbeat tone. This introduction does not follow the usual drill; instead, it brings both bad and good news. First, the bad:

I have been observing the megasuccesses on Wall Street for almost a decade, long enough to convince me that there are four barriers which prevent most of us from ever becoming really astute investors.

1) **Time.** This sounds fatuous, but being good at anything—including managing money—takes time. And I mean real time, not just a bunch of days here and there, but rather huge chunks of time spent reading, crunching numbers, and talking to experts. So unless you're willing to make a serious and ongoing commitment, count time as an insurmountable hurdle.

2) **Practice.** This sounds scary, but practice means being willing to try a little bit of everything to see what—if any—your skills are. That means investing in exotica like hog bellies and games of chance like initial public offerings, along with the more routine ways of getting yourself wet like buying blue chip stocks. Unless you are a natural risk lover with tons of money to lose, this is also a hard barrier to jump.

3) **Experience.** This is another piece of fatuous advice, but being more than a fifteen-minute wonder requires sitting through both a bull and a bear cycle. In a bull market, when all investments seem to pan out, experience is what prepares you for the fact that it's bound to end; and in a bear market,

when nothing seems to work, experience is what comforts you that this, too, shall pass. Without this kind of experience, you will be prey to the mood extremes that make for an erratic investment record, one where ups are canceled out by downs. And that's not the way to get ahead in this game. So unless you have the patience to have your patience tried, count this as another insurmountable obstacle.

4) **Firmness of character.** A true toughie. There's the regular and easier-to-come-by firmness with which you motor your broker off the phone before he or she can sell you another tax shelter. And then there's real firmness of character—the discipline to sell something both when it is going your way and when it is not. In the former case, that means selling instead of waiting to make a teensy bit more money; and in the latter, it means selling instead of waiting until the mother recovers enough to put you even. If you're the type who scarfs down the frosting before eating the cake, forget firmness of character.

(None of these conditions, you may have noted, has anything to do with intelligence. In fact, I suspect that in some financial endeavors, like currency trading, intelligence is a handicap. And none of these barriers is permanent: People do change.)

Anyway, here is the bad news in one dose: Not only do you need time, self-confidence, and resoluteness to be a truly successful investor, but this book (sadly) can't help you develop these traits.

Now for the good news: What this book *can* help you do is pierce the seemingly unpierceable thicket of jargon used to describe the action in money and finance. To be sure, practitioners in most fields surround themselves with verbiage designed to keep out the uninitiated. But this seems to be especially true of Wall Street. Everyone—from slick-talking brokers to pompous-pronouncing investment bankers to foul-mouthed traders—uses the kind of vocabulary employed by short-order cooks. Colorful, but impenetrable to outsiders.

To make this shorthand (the expletives deleted) understand-able, all the entries were written to stand alone. However, if you are looking for a broader understanding of something like zero coupon bonds, then follow the directions to "*See* BOND, BOND YIELD" at the end of the ZERO COUPON BOND entry and read on.

Likewise, there is no explicit how-to advice—like which is a better investment, a ninety-day certificate of deposit or a two-year U.S. Treasury bond—because the correct answer depends on variables known only to you. If, however, you read the entries on bonds, bond yields, certificates of deposit, Treasury securities, and interest, then you should have enough information to make a more informed decision. (That is, you should be better able to make an informed decision after taking personal variables like your tax bracket, your liquidity needs, and how comfy you are with risk into consideration.)

Astute readers will notice that some entries appeared in my first book, *ABZs of Economics*. This repetition is due not to laziness, but to the wish that each book be complete in itself. Thus, the ideas that are basic to understanding both economics and money and finance appear in both books. (For example, knowing what exactly the Federal Reserve does is crucial for public policy questions as well as for investment decisions.) I have customized some of the repeat entries so they address money matters more directly. Some, however, are as they were in my first book because, modestly put, I couldn't improve on them.

And finally, this book was written to be true to the best one-sentence advice I've come across in my years as a financial journalist and stock market columnist: Be cynical in all things. Note that this advice goes one step farther than an injunction to be skeptical, and it's a crucial step: It's the one which goes the longest way toward protecting your money.

Susan Lee
New York City

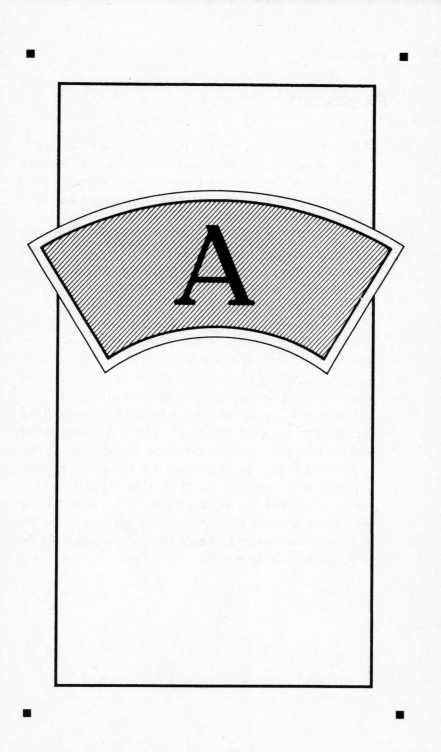

ACQUISITION

A type of merger in which one firm takes over another firm.

The process usually involves the acquiring firm buying a large chunk of the target firm's common stock, thereby gaining a controlling interest in the target firm. That might not sound exactly thrilling, but it can be.

If the target firm's management doesn't wish to be acquired —and resists—the result can be a marvelously mean-spirited battle: The target firm's management will be characterized as self-seeking and incompetent, while the acquiring firm, or group of investors, will be called irresponsible predators.

Moreover, acquisitions can be remunerative if you hold shares in the target firm. If the acquiring firm buys a large chunk of stock quickly, it will push up the value of the stock. Also, the acquiring firm will often offer to buy out current shareholders at a price which is above the market price.

Companies acquire firms for a variety of reasons. If the target company's stock is thought to be underpriced by the market, then acquisition is a cheap way for the acquiring firm to grow bigger. If the target company is in the same or a related business, then acquisition might be a clever way to achieve "synergy," in which the resulting whole will be better than the sum of the separate parts. And the tax situation of the two firms might also create a synergy, lowering the tax bite for the acquiring firm. *See* MERGER.

Adr

This entry is to forestall confusion. The letters ADR can be an abbreviation for any of three unrelated things.

ADR may mean automatic dividend reinvestment (where dividends are automatically reinvested into the stock of the paying corporation). ADR may also mean asset depreciation range, a type of accelerated depreciation. And finally, ADR may mean American Depository Receipts, certificates of ownership for foreign stocks which trade in the United States; these ADRs are issued by U.S. banks.

Affiliated company

A company of which a significant portion—but less than half—of the stock is owned by another company.

American stock exchange

Marketplace located in New York City where people gather to trade financial instruments like stocks and bonds.

There are a bunch of stock exchanges in the United States. In terms of size and influence, the American Stock Exchange falls somewhere between the biggest and best known, the New York Stock Exchange, and the several regional exchanges in Boston, Philadelphia, and the Pacific coast. Companies which are listed for trading on the American Stock Exchange are, by and large, smaller and less well known than those which qualify for listing on the New York Stock Exchange. *See* NEW YORK STOCK EXCHANGE; OVER-THE-COUNTER MARKET; STOCK EXCHANGE.

AMORTIZE, AMORTIZATION

The process of extinguishing a debt.

While there's nothing wrong with that definition, there's a lot more to be said. If the debt is a loan, then amortization refers to the installment payments which cover the interest on the loan, although it might also include payments of the principal. If the debt is a home mortgage, then amortization usually refers to both interest and principal. (And the mortgage is thus said to be "fully amortized.")

For firms, amortization has three guises. Generally, it means that the firm is allocating the cost of an asset over its estimated useful life; specifically, however, it can appear as "depreciation" when the asset is part of plant, property, or equipment; it can appear as "depletion" when the asset is a natural resource (like an oil reserve); and it can appear as "amortization" when the asset is intangible (like goodwill).

ANNUAL REPORT

A yearly report to stockholders from management.

An annual report must include the auditor's report and various financial statements describing the health of the firm. But annual reports from most companies, particularly big corporations, include a lot more: color portraits of the management team, a carefully worded text emphasizing the year's triumphs (and perhaps explaining the defeats), and arty photos of the company in action. In short, an annual report is also a piece of slick public relations. *See* FINANCIAL STATEMENTS.

ANNUITY

A series of payments, usually made at regular intervals over a specified period of time.

Annuities are often purchased from insurance companies as a form of old-age insurance; that is, annuity payments are supposed to substitute for paychecks after retirement. In this case, the annuitant pays a lump sum to the insurance company and the company invests that money, hoping to provide the annuity payments out of its investment returns. An annuity, then, is a contract under which the company promises to make payments on whatever terms have been agreed to. Terms? Lots of choices:

Annuities can be "certain," which means that the payments continue for a fixed amount of time, or they can be "life," which means they end with the death of the annuitant. Annuities can be "immediate," which means payments start right away, or they can be "deferred," which means payments begin at a future date.

As for the payments themselves, they can either be a fixed amount agreed to at the beginning of the contract or a variable amount which depends on how successful the annuity-giver is in investing the annuitant's lump sum. There is risk in either arrangement. When the payments are fixed, the risk assumed by the company is that it must deliver on its promise no matter how poorly it manages the money; the risk assumed by the annuitant is that inflation may erode the purchasing power of the payments. When the payments are variable, more risk is assumed by the annuitant—if returns on the company's investment portfolio are small, the payments will be, too. (On the other hand, if returns are big, the size of the payments will be gratifying.)

The price of an annuity depends on whether the payments are at a fixed or variable rate and whether the payments are for a specified period of time or for the life of the annuitant.

APPRECIATION (ASSETS)

When the market value of an asset increases.

Many assets are bought with the express—and fervent—hope that their value will go up: stocks, bonds, real estate, jewelry, artwork. Until they're sold, however, any appreciation is on paper only and "not realized." Nitty-gritty appreciation occurs when the asset is sold or the "value is realized."

APPRECIATION (CURRENCY)

A rise in the value of a currency relative to other currencies.

Under a system of floating exchange rates, the market sets

the value of currencies. A nation with a "strong" currency—one which other nations wish to own—will see its currency rise in value relative to other currencies. The nation with the appreciating currency, however, will usually find itself eventually running a trade deficit as its exports become more expensive and its imports become cheaper. Politically, a country takes pride in having a strong currency—that is, until its trade deficit means that domestic businesses are being priced out of foreign markets. When that happens, the country will usually depreciate its currency. *See* DEPRECIATION (CURRENCY); DEVALUATION; FOREIGN EXCHANGE.

ARBITRAGE

A sophisticated version of buying cheap and selling dear.

Arbitrage involves buying something in one market and simultaneously (or almost) selling it for more money in another market. Arbitraging is usually done in the rarified high-tech world of foreign currency markets or the spot markets for commodities, where price discrepancies can be found and transactions can be completed in a matter of seconds. In other words, it's usually done by professionals. Nonetheless, arbitrage can be done by anyone plucky—and lucky—enough to spot a favorable price discrepancy.

The opportunity to arbitrage is what brings prices in various markets more or less into line: That is, when traders remove supply from cheap markets, prices there will go up, and when traders deliver supply to expensive markets, prices in that market will go down. Thus, arbitraging tends to equalize prices in all markets.

Note that the practice of arbitragers is different from the practice of those who are called by the more elegant name arbitrageurs. The latter, also known as arbs, argue that they too are in the business of spotting price discrepancies in stocks. That is, they identify companies whose stock is undervalued by the market, buy big blocks of that stock, wait until the price is pushed up by bargain hunters making a takeover bid, and then sell their stock for—reportedly—high profits.

That's what they argue, anyway. The truth is that some arbs simply act on insider information. They hear of impending takeovers, usually from people involved in the deal—like bankers or lawyers—and then take big positions in the target company. Acting on this type of insider information is, of course, against the law.

ASSET

Physical or intangible property that has potential value.

The formal designation "assets" found on business balance sheets typically takes two forms. One is current assets like cash or things that can be quickly turned into cash. The other is tangible assets, or fixed assets like buildings and equipment. But assets can also be intangible, like copyrights and patents.

Assets appear on the left-hand side of the balance sheet, liabilities on the right. In fact, the reason balance sheets are called balance sheets is because assets always equal liabilities.

Individuals, too, can draw up balance sheets. Here again,

assets typically take two forms: nonfinancial items like houses, land, autos, and refrigerators, and financial items like savings accounts, pensions, stocks, and bonds. *See* BALANCE SHEET; LIABILITY.

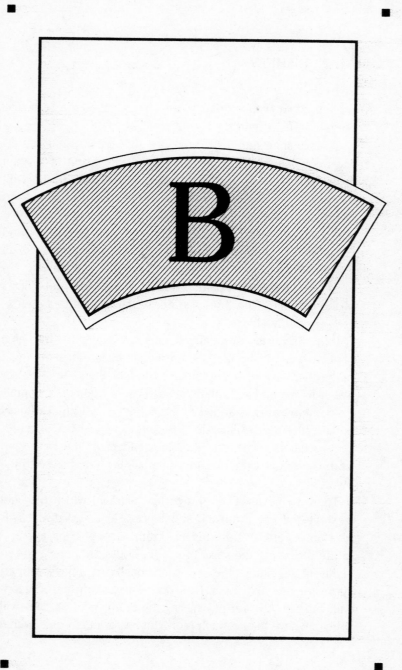

BALANCE SHEET

Document showing a firm's assets and liabilities at a particular point in time, usually the end of the year.

Balance sheets are called balance sheets because assets always equal liabilities. Consider the balance sheet of a small firm, the Framistan Company. Assets consist of all the stuff Framistan owns—cash on hand, accounts receivable from framistans sold, inventories of both materials to make framistans and framistans made but not sold, and the factory and equipment needed to make framistans. Liabilities consist of all the stuff Framistan owes—accounts payable to suppliers, salaries owed but not yet paid to workers, managers, and officers of the company, the mortgage on the factory, and, of course, any outstanding loans.

If the Framistan Company is a healthy enterprise, the value of its assets will be larger than its liabilities. But that would make the balance sheet unbalanced. So the difference between assets and liabilities, called owners' equity (or sloppily called net worth), is added to the liability side to make things equal. Why the liability side? Because owners' equity represents what is owned by the stockholders in the Framistan Company; thus, owners' equity is a liability—it is owed to the owners.

There is, however, one important element which may not be reflected on Framistan's balance sheet—goodwill. This pleasant-sounding entry reflects Framistan's past success and future prospects: the spirit of its employees, the utter respectability of its name, the good relationship it enjoys with its suppliers and customers. How does one put a price on goodwill? Simple. A buyer purchasing the Framistan Company will probably have to pay much more than its owners' equity—that additional sum is then called goodwill and will be carried on the balance sheet.

The Framistan Company is a very stripped-down example. The balance sheet of a larger company, or one with fancy accountants, contains many more categories. Assets could include marketable securities and other investments; liabilities could include dividends payable and accrued taxes. And owners' equity could include the par value of preferred and common stock, along with retained earnings. Indeed, the balance sheets of very large—or very wily—corporations often come with pages and pages of footnotes to explain each entry.

Balloon payment

When the final payment in a series of payments is larger than the preceding ones. Balloon payments are often found billowing out from home mortgages.

Bank failure

A polite way of describing a bankrupt bank.

Banks are heavily regulated institutions—both their borrowing and lending practices are subject to scrutiny by state and federal agencies. Nonetheless, there are dozens and dozens of ways for banks to get into trouble. They can make a bunch of bad loans and thus not have enough money coming in; they can pay too much interest to attract deposits and thus have too much money going out. Or they can fail because officers or staff engage in criminal mischief, like embezzling.

A bank is said to fail when it becomes insolvent—when it doesn't have enough assets to cover its liabilities. But a bank failure can be an elusive event. Bank regulators can prop up a technically insolvent bank by pumping in fresh money, or they can issue pieces of paper that banks can carry on their balance sheets as assets; or—the preferred option—they can "merge" the failed bank with a healthy bank. Presto! No bank failure.

Before the 1930s, when bank regulatory agencies were established, a bank failure was a serious event. Back then, a failed bank was a failed bank. It closed its doors, leaving its depositors out in the cold—often literally. Back then, even a rumor that a bank was in trouble was enough to panic depositors of that bank, and even other banks, into withdrawing their funds. That, of course, only exacerbated the situation so that healthy banks fell along with the troubled one. (This sequence of events was called a "bank panic" or a "run on the banks.")

Nowadays, however, bank regulators and deposit insurance have made the fallout from a bank failure fairly routine. Nowadays, the only activity such an event excites are editorials frothing and foaming about the irresponsibility (kind) or the stupidity (less kind) of the bank's management.

BANKRUPTCY

When an individual or corporation is legally declared insolvent by a court of law. A declaration of bankruptcy is more than just a statement, however. Insolvency doesn't usually describe a situation as mean as flat broke, but rather one in which liabilities are greater than assets. In other words, there are enough assets to pay back some, but not all, debts. And that's where bankruptcy proceedings come in.

Bankruptcy is actually a process by which the assets of the bankruptee are transferred to a court-appointed official. The official then liquidates the assets and makes sure that creditors with legal priority (the Internal Revenue Service, for example) get paid off before the rest of the creditors and that the creditors are all treated fairly. Bankruptcy comes in two varieties, voluntary and involuntary. Individuals or corporations can declare themselves bankrupt, or creditors can get together and petition the court to declare a bankruptcy.

BANKS AND BANKING

Commercial banks are very important players from a financial point of view. When the banking system works the way it's supposed to, banks act as financial intermediaries, provide liquidity to the financial system, and serve as the conduit for the nation's monetary policy. These are three fairly distinct functions, so consider:

Financial intermediaries. Granted, a description of the modern banking system can get a little tedious, but it's not at all complicated. Financial intermediation involves nothing more than linking up people who want to save money with people who want to spend it. Savers put their money in banks; banks, in turn, lend the money to spenders. Without this financial intermediation, savings might rest idly under mattresses and borrowers would not be able to buy the goods and services that make the economy go round. Clearly, then, financial intermediation is crucial for a healthy, sophisticated economy.

In order to perform intermediation, banks must offer savers inducements to put their money in bank accounts rather than under mattresses. Banks make it worthwhile for savers to become lenders in several ways. For starters, banks offer a convenient and safe place to stash cash. Customers deposit their money—open an account—and receive checks which substitute for cash. Banks also offer savers a rate of return (interest) on their money, making banks a better deal than mattresses.

After luring savers into depositing their money, banks transform them into lenders by allowing borrowers to use the funds. Banks make borrowers pay for this privilege by charging interest on loan money.

If all goes according to plan, banks pay savers less interest on deposits than they charge borrowers for loans. Banks use this "spread" to pay for their expenses, and anything left over constitutes profit. In this respect, then, financial intermediation depends on banks being able to borrow cheap and lend dear.

Financial intermediation covers a lot of transactions. On the savers' side, it encompasses everything from modest, long-term passbook accounts to the immodest sums deposited overnight by large corporations. On the borrowers' side, it encompasses modest, short-term consumer loans to immodest, long-term loans to foreign governments.

Liquidity. Banks are important players in the creation of money. While banks can't print it—only the federal government can do that—they can do something almost as neat.

Consider what happens when a saver makes a bank deposit. The amount of the deposit, say $1,000, appears on the bank's balance sheet as a liability: the bank owes the money to the depositor. However, the bank doesn't keep 100 percent cash against the deposit, but only a fraction of it. The bank reserves a fraction, say 10 percent, of the initial deposit and lends out the rest. (Since loans are carried on the bank's balance sheet as assets, the $1,000 deposit liability will be balanced by $100 in cash and $900 in loan assets.)

This transaction is the heart of money creation. The bank makes the loan by opening an account for the borrower from which the borrower may draw cash or write a check, which comes to the same thing. In other words, the bank has used the first depositor's account to create $900 in a second account.

But money creation doesn't stop there. Presumably, the borrower will withdraw the money on the new account to pay for whatever he or she wished to borrow the money for. That money will then go into a third depositor's account. Again, the bank will reserve 10 percent of that deposit as $90 in cash and lend the rest, $810, to another borrower. Presto! Another $810 has been added to the supply of money. And so it goes, involving many depositors and their banks, until the created money becomes too small to measure. (In this example, the initial $1,000 deposit can create up to $10,000—$9,000 in the form of loans, and $1,000 as cash reserves.) The fractional reserve system thus allows banks to increase the money supply.

Conduit for monetary policy. The Federal Reserve Board, the nation's central bank, determines the course of monetary policy. But after having determined what to do—allow more money into the economy or take some out—it must use the commercial banking system to implement its decision.

Essentially the Fed can use the banks in two ways: by changing the reserve requirement or by engaging in something called open-market operations. If, for example, the Fed requires banks to reserve 10 percent in cash against every deposit, it can then pump more money into the system by lowering that requirement to 5 percent. In other words, by permitting banks to loan out 95 percent of deposits (as opposed to 90 percent) the Fed can make more money available to circulate through the economy.

Open-market operations are just as straightforward. Here the Fed either buys or sells government bonds. If the Fed wants less money in the economy, it will sell government bonds, knowing that the buyers will pay for those bonds with checks drawn on the banking system. The Fed then presents those checks to the banks for payment, thus removing some money from circulation. (Technically, the Fed removes the money by "cashing" the check from the bank's reserves held at the Fed. With less reserves to back up its deposits, the bank's lending activities are thus constrained.) *See* THE FED.

Barter

Obtaining goods or services without using money. Without using *money?* Sure. Money is a latecomer to the world of trading things. Primitive people satisfied their covetous impulses by exchanging things like feathers for things like skins, just as kids now trade baseball cards. Whatever could be owned could be used to buy ownership of something else.

But as civilization moved on, barter became too complicated to move with it. In fact, barter did itself in by encouraging specialization in production: If I produce super tomatoes and you produce great broccoli, it makes sense for each of us to specialize and then trade our veggies. But specialization makes us less able to satisfy our other needs. If, for example, a sudden craving for bananas strikes, both of us will have to find a banana farmer to gratify our desires. But what if the banana farmer hates broccoli and is allergic to tomatoes? We then have to hunt around for a farmer who not only wants to trade her produce for our broccoli or tomatoes but grows something that the banana farmer wants. The remedy for ever more cumbersome barter arrangements was the invention of a medium of exchange—money.

All these difficulties notwithstanding, barter has made a comeback in these presumably nonprimitive times. Whether it's an informal trade of my handknit sweater for your plumbing services or a more formal organization where potential traders advertise their goods or services, bartering can be cheaper than using the money economy. No need to pay for the services of a middleman, and no need to pay taxes.

Barter is also done by businesses and countries. Indeed, barter is very popular with governments of planned economies. Barter allows these nations to trade the stuff they regularly overproduce for stuff they regularly need, and all without having to use the hard currency of which they regularly have a shortage. *See* MONEY.

BASIS POINT

A measure for interest rates and bond yields.

One basis point equals one-hundredth of a percent (.01 percent). If, for example, an investor wanted to express the spread (or difference) in a bond yielding 10.00 percent and another one yielding 10.10 percent, he or she would say there's a spread of ten basis points. Now, such a small difference might seem like quibbling, but consider the ramifications of ten basis points when there is big money involved. If the investment is $100 million in bonds, the spread amounts to $100,000. That's a rather handsome sum to ignore.

BATH (*or, often,* BIG BATH)

What is said to happen when an individual or a firm recognizes a bad investment decision by liquidating it.

For individuals, the definition of a bath can be fairly casual. Selling a stock at loss, for example, might prompt: "Boy, did I take a bath on that one!" For firms, baths usually take place on the balance sheet when they write off an asset in which they made a big investment, such as a line of business. Firms take big baths to avoid taking the smaller baths involved in a gradual write-down of a failure. Big baths are often taken by new management to make its regime look better on future balance sheets.

BEAR

Hold on, this is a rather long definition: An individual who thinks that the price of a stock—or a bond, currency, or commodity—is going to fall and who accordingly sells that stock (without actually owning it) by "borrowing" it from a brokerage house. The profit comes when the individual buys the stock later, at a lower price, to replace the borrowed stock he or she has already sold. (Not to belabor the point, this maneuver, called short selling, is the same as the classic way to profit on the stock market—buying low and selling high—only the process is reversed. Here you sell first and buy later.)

That is the precise definition. The term "bearish," however, is used to describe anybody who is pessimistic about prices, whether or not he or she actually sells anything short. The term "bear market" refers to a market with falling prices. And the term "bear raid" is what's said to happen when short sellers run around bad-mouthing a stock, hoping to push its price down. The term "bear" comes from the practice of bearskin jobbers, who sell the skin before they shoot the bear. *See* BULL; SHORT.

Beta coefficient

A measure of how closely price movements in an individual stock correspond with movements in the overall stock market.

A stock with a high beta is riskier than one with a low beta. For example, a high-beta stock—usually called an aggressive or growth stock—could mightily outperform the averages in an up market but miserably underperform in a down market. A low-beta stock—usually called a defensive stock—could rise less than the market in an up year, but would fall less than the market in a down year. In other words, the returns from a high-beta stock can go from thrillingly high to depressingly low, while the returns from a low-beta stock will plod along.

Calculating betas is a complicated business, but an important one for investors concerned about risk. Granted, all investments carry risk, but some are riskier than others. Say the stock market goes up 1 percent and Framistan's stock goes up 2 percent. Framistan is then said to have a beta of two and is considered riskier than stocks with betas of less than two.

BLOCK TRADE

A securities transaction which involves at least 10,000 shares. Block refers to the number of shares bought or sold by a single party—it means a large chunk. *See* ODD LOT.

BLUE CHIP

Shares of common stock in any big, well-known company which has the reputation of paying its dividends year in and year out. The price of a blue chip is usually higher than its yield would justify. Why? Because investors are willing to pay a premium for the lower risk associated with bigness and predictability.

BOND

A long-term debt instrument. Long-term means anything over ten years. Bonds are also called fixed-income securities because they promise to make regular payments to the bond owner at a fixed rate of interest.

The issuer of a bond is the borrower; the buyer of a bond is the creditor. Bonds can be issued by the federal government, by state or local governments (in which case they're called municipal bonds), by foreign governments, or by corporations.

Bonds come in several varieties:

They can be secured, which means they are backed by a specific asset (like mortgage bonds), or they can be unsecured (like debentures). They can be traded in for stocks (convertible bonds). And—this is sneaky—they can be callable, which means that the issuer can redeem them before their maturity date.

Bonds used to be considered very safe, boring investments. You paid your money and clipped your coupons. No more. The bout of gyrating interest rates in the 1980s made investing in bonds more exciting. And less safe—a return of 10 percent, which looks hunky-dory today, might look really dumb in three years if interest rates spike up to 15 percent. *See* BASIS POINT; BOND YIELD; INTEREST; YIELD CURVE.

Bond yield

The return on an investment in bonds.

Let's say you can buy a ten-year bond which is worth $1,000 at maturity (its face value) but sells for $900 (the market price) and carries a 5 percent annual coupon. I'll explain why the market price differs from the face value later, but for now consider the yield embedded in the coupon rate. The coupon rate is fixed—it is the rate of interest which will be paid to you every year. (It's called the coupon rate because some bonds actually come equipped with coupons which can be clipped and presented for money on their due dates.) A coupon rate of 5 percent on a $1,000 bond means the buyer will get 5 percent of the $1,000, or $50, each year.

But the coupon rate doesn't tell the full story. Consider, then, what's called the current yield.

The current yield is the annual dollar return divided by the market price of the bond. After all, since you can buy a $1,000 bond for only $900, that price gap should be considered as part of the return on the bond. In this case, the current yield would be 5.56 percent. Aha, that sounds better than the 5 percent coupon, and it is. But wait, it gets still better.

The current yield covers only the first year's return on the bond and neglects the $100 capital gain when you cash the bond in for $1,000. So consider now a third type of yield—the yield to maturity, sometimes called the effective yield.

In this case, the yield to maturity is 6.4 percent. That's even better than the current yield because it includes all the coupon payments you are entitled to, discounted over ten years. (Discounting is a way of recognizing that $50 a year from now will be worth more than $50 today because over that year the $50 will earn interest; likewise, $50 two years from now will be worth more than $50 one year from now, and so on.)

The discounting formula also takes into account the $1,000 you will receive in year ten, when the bond can be cashed in. In fact, the market price of the bond, $900, follows from the discount rate—it is the present (current) value of a $1,000 bond which yields 6.4 percent over ten years.

The fact that both the current and effective yields are above the 5 percent coupon rate brings us back to the question of why the market price and the face value of bonds can differ.

If interest rates were absolutely stable and coupons paid out every day, that would be the end of it. A $1,000 bond would sell for $1,000, and the coupon rate, current yield, and yield to maturity would all be identical. But interest rates are not stable, and coupons don't pay out every day, so the valuation of bonds is a dynamic exercise.

Consider our bond with a face value of $1,000 and a coupon rate of 5 percent. These two things never change. What changes, of course, are economic circumstances—most important, interest rates—which, in turn, will change the bond's market price and its effective yield.

Bond prices and yields are inversely related. If interest rates go up, bond prices go down and vice versa. Why? Let's say that interest rates rise to 7 percent. Now, that's above our bond's 6.4 percent effective yield. Since nobody would want to buy a bond with a yield below 7 percent, and since neither the face value nor the coupon rate can change, that leaves only one price that can vary in order to bring the effective yield up to 7 percent—the market price of the bond.

In this case, the price of the bond would have to fall from $900 to $858 in order to bring its yield up to 7 percent. In other words, the present (current) value of our bond must fall to account for a rise in interest rates above 6.4 percent. That's common sense: If you can earn the market rate of interest of 7 percent in another investment, the price of our bond must fall to induce you to buy its 5 percent coupons.

Moreover, the value of a bond will rise as the time for its coupon to pay out draws near, even if interest rates don't budge. Why? Simple—the seller will be forfeiting the $50 payment and the buyer will be receiving the right to collect that $50, so the price of the bond will rise accordingly to reflect that event. So, too, the value of the bond will get closer to its face value as its maturity draws near because, as payout time approaches, changes in interest rates and effective yields become less important.

This example explains why the market price of a bond falls below its face value when interest rates go up; in this case, the bond is said to be selling "below par" or "at a discount." If, on the other hand, interest rates fall below the coupon rate, then the price of the bond will rise above its face value; the bond is said to be selling "above par" or "at a premium." *See* YIELD CURVE; ZERO COUPON BOND.

BOOK VALUE

Several meanings here. When the words "book value" appear on a firm's balance sheet, they measure the value of an asset, usually at its historical cost (the price paid when it was acquired). When book value is used to measure the worth of a firm ("total book value"), it means the value of total assets minus total liabilities. And finally, "book value per share of common stock" is the net worth of a firm divided by the number of shares of outstanding. *See* NET WORTH.

BROKER

Financial intermediary (go-between) who links up buyers and sellers.

In stocks, for example, a broker arranges a trade between

the buyer and the seller ("executing the order") and then charges a commission, or fee, for performing that service.

Bull

Strictly speaking, a bull is any individual who thinks the price of a stock—or a bond, commodity, or currency—will go up and who accordingly buys the stock, expecting to profit by selling it later at a higher price. (A bull who buys a stock is said to be "long" on the stock as opposed to a bear, who sells the stock "short.")

Less strictly speaking, a person is said to be "bullish" if he is optimistic about prices, whether or not he actually buys anything. And a "bull market" is one in which prices are generally rising.

Whether it's basic human nature to be optimistic or whether it's because the financial community makes lots of money selling securities, people on Wall Street tend to be bullish. Just ask your broker . . . *See* BEAR.

Business cycle

The technical term for the ups and downs in the economic growth rate. Although the word "cycle" implies some regular, rhythmic movement, business cycles are erratic. They encompass varying periods of time—the ups have ranged anywhere from nine months to eight years, the downs from half a year to six years—and they vary in plenitude and severity. Their only true cyclical aspect is that ups are followed by downs which are, in turn, followed by ups.

Business cycle chat employs some specific terms: The lowest point, which occurs during a recession (or depression) is called a trough; the highest point, which occurs during a boom, is called a peak. The in-between periods are called expansions and contractions.

The economic statistic used to track business cycles is the trend (or historical) growth rate of the gross national product, minus inflation. When the GNP falls below its trend, economists say the economy is contracting; when it grows above its trend, the economy is expanding. The long-term trend of GNP, by the way, is gently upwards, a reflection of the fact that periods of expansion have been longer and stronger than periods of contraction.

Ideally, of course, there would be no downs. Ideally, economists and politicians would be able to manipulate the economy to ensure steady growth without reversals. Realistically, however, the economy is not all that manageable.

Most obviously, it is prey to events beyond the control of economists. These events are called, appropriately enough, shocks. Inflationary shocks, for example, can be particularly menacing to economists' dreams of stable prices. Consider the weather, a traditional wild card: Floods or droughts can translate into a bad harvest which, in turn, means suddenly higher food prices.

Almost as obviously, the economy is also prey to events orchestrated by its players. A giant tax increase, for example, might curtail spending severely, causing economic activity to sicken. Or a burst of production from overly optimistic firms might propel the economy into an "inventory slowdown," as firms then find they must cut back to avoid being swamped with unsold goods.

Some investors try to take advantage of the business cycle by investing in industries which are likely to do well at particular periods in the cycle. For example, at the beginning of an up cycle, such an investor might buy housing stocks because good times in the housing industry tend to lead good times in the economy. When the economic expansion is underway, he or she might sell housing and shift into consumer-oriented goods stocks because this sector closely tracks economic growth. When the economy starts showing signs of slowing down, these investors might sell consumer goods stocks and buy shares in capital goods companies because flush times in this sector tend to lag behind the economy. And then, when the down phase threatens, these investors might sell their capital goods stocks and just sit on their cash, waiting for the next up phase to begin.

BUYER'S MARKET

Situation in which supply is temporarily greater than demand at current prices.

When demand is inadequate or buyers are scarce, sellers compete for buyers by lowering their prices. Thus, a buyer's market is characterized by falling prices. In other words, a buyer's market is good for buyers and bad for sellers.

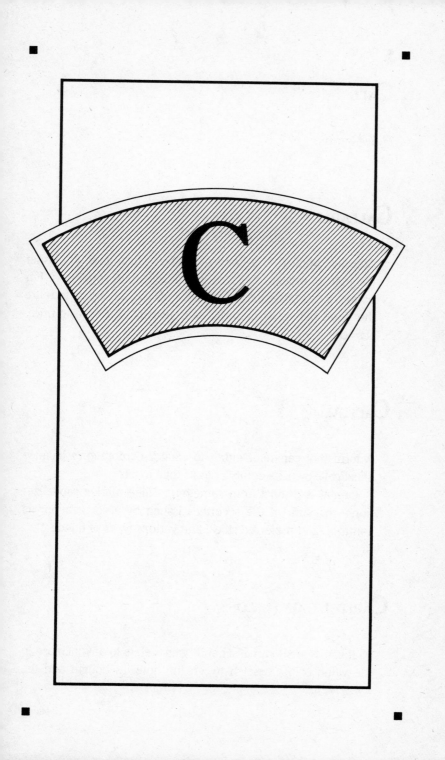

CALL

See OPTION.

CALLABLE

Adjective applied to a bond or a stock which gives the issuer the right to redeem the security under certain conditions. For bonds, a call provision, or privilege, allows the issuer to retire the bond before its maturity date, usually at a specific price. *See* BOND.

CAPITAL

A term that can refer either to what a corporation's balance sheet calls owner's equity or to its total assets.

Capital is distinct from something called market capitalization—the sum of the securities issued by a corporation, its common and preferred stock, and various types of bonds.

CAPITAL GAIN (*or* LOSS)

"Capital" refers to an asset and "gain" refers to any increase in the value of the asset between the time it's bought and the time it's sold. (A capital loss is what happens when the asset is sold for less money than you paid for it.) Strictly speaking, the asset must be sold before a gain or loss can occur, otherwise it's all just "on paper."

CAPITAL MARKET

The financial market for long-term investment and savings. Like other markets, the capital market serves to link up buyers and sellers. In this case, sellers are individuals, businesses, and governments wishing to raise funds (capital), while buyers are individuals, businesses, and governments wishing to save money.

The financial instruments through which this linkage takes place are varied. They include corporate stocks and bonds; residential, commercial, and farm mortgages; federal, state, and local government bonds; and even consumer and business loans. These instruments also vary in length from a year to several decades, making the capital market distinct from the money market, where instruments are very short-term, sometimes even overnight. And finally, the capital market has two tiers: There's the new issue market, where financial instruments make their debut, and there's the secondary market, where those instruments are traded after their debut.

A healthy capital market—one which permits lots of buying and selling of many different instruments—is essential to a healthy economy.

Take, for example, a corporation wanting to build a new factory. First, it would be mighty unusual to have all the necessary cash on hand, so the money must be borrowed. Second, the company wants to make the best use of its resources, so it needs flexibility in the way it borrows. Third, such a construction project takes a long time, so the company needs to be sure the money won't run out before the project is completed. And fourth, lenders want to be assured that their investment is liquid (that they can sell the company's financial instruments to other investors), so they want a secondary market with lots of buyers.

In other words, the corporation needs a market in which a large amount of money can be raised in a number of ways for a long-term investment, and investors and lenders need a market which can absorb whatever amount of money they want to invest for however long they want to invest it. Both need an efficient capital market. And so does the economy. Absent such a market, the corporation might not be able to build a new factory, thus expanding its production and creating new jobs, and so on and so forth. *See* MONEY MARKET.

CAPITALIZED VALUE, CAPITALIZATION RATE

Other terms for DISCOUNTING.

CASH

To an individual, "cash" usually means cash money, or bills and coins. To an accountant, cash means cash money, bank deposits, and negotiable checks.

Cash flow

The amount of money coming into a firm (its receipts) minus the amount of money going out of the firm (its expenditures).

There are a number of ways to look at a company's cash flow: before and after taxes, for example. But the way most familiar to investors is something called the "statement of sources and uses of cash" or "statement of changes in financial position," which appears as part of a company's annual report.

Needless to say, firms like to have a "positive" cash flow (more money coming in than going out). Investors, too, like firms with strong cash flows. Not only can such a firm afford to pay its creditors, suppliers, and workers, it can also afford to keep up its dividend payments. Nonetheless, even well-run companies can experience cash shortages if they're expanding and must borrow money, or if there is a lag between production expenditures and sales revenues. Firms experiencing a negative cash flow must usually go out and borrow funds.

Certificate of deposit

A claim issued by a bank whereby the bank promises to pay a specified rate of interest on a specified amount of money over the specified life of the certificate.

The key here, as you might have guessed, is the word "specified." If a depositor wants to withdraw the money before the certificate comes due, he or she could pay a penalty or forfeit some interest. (There is, however, a secondary market for the sale of outstanding CDs to which cash-needy investors can turn.)

Rates on CDs are competitively set. And since they are a major source of funds for most banks, banks are usually quite aggressive in persuading people to buy their paper—hence those familiar advertisements in local newspapers for high-yield CDs at nonlocal banks.

Investing in CDs is generally considered a low-risk investment because they are deposits at banks and bank deposits are insured by the federal government. True. Except for deposits over $100,000. And, every so often, a bank will go bankrupt and leave the $100,000-plus CD holders holding, well, the bag.

CHURNING

Colorful, if somewhat negative, word to describe the frequent buying and selling of assets.

Churning is typically used to describe what stockbrokers do when they persuade clients to buy and sell securities at a clip faster than the return on their clients' account justifies. That is, the continuous turnover generates more in commission fees for the broker than it does in profits for the client.

That having been said—with high moral tone—there are two additional points to be made. Some investors churn their own portfolios without any help from brokers; those, for example, who are forever yanking their money out of one bank's certificate of deposit to put it in another bank's certificate of deposit, or who are constantly switching their money from mutual fund X to mutual fund Y. Too, churning is not always bad; there are some investors who can turn over all the assets in their portfolios several times a year and still make lots of money net of transaction costs.

Closed-End Mutual Fund *or* CLOSED-END INVESTMENT COMPANY

An investment entity which is both a company and a fund. It's like a company in that management sells stock in itself to raise capital or borrows money from banks; it's like a mutual fund in that its capital is then invested in other things.

Closed-end mutual funds, just like the more popular open-end mutual funds, have stated investment objectives: Some will invest only in common stocks, others in commodities, still others are balanced (a little of everything).

Since there are a fixed number outstanding, shares in investment companies trade like any other company shares on an exchange or over the counter, and their value is set by the market. While the share value is closely related to the value of the underlying net assets, it can—and often does—deviate. If, for example, the market thinks that management is incompetent, then shares will trade at a price lower than the value of the underlying portfolio; if the market thinks that management is shrewd, then shares will trade at a value higher than the portfolio. *See* OPEN-END MUTUAL FUND.

CLOSELY HELD CORPORATION *or* CLOSED CORPORATION

A business in which most or all of the stock is owned by a small group of people who are usually also in management positions.

COMMERCIAL PAPER

Unsecured promissory notes of large, usually extremely credit-worthy, firms. These notes are also usually very short-term, for very large sums of money—say, a ninety-day note for $1 million—and they carry interest rates which are below prime rates. *See* PRIME RATE.

COMMISSION

The cut, usually a percentage of the value of the transaction, taken by a middleman for performing a service—as in stockbroker's commission, real estate broker's commission, or investment banker's commission.

Commodity

A relatively homogeneous item, usually a raw material, that is for sale. That doesn't sound like a big deal, and it isn't. The big deal comes when commodities are for sale on a commodity exchange. Serious stuff—no joke.

A commodity exchange is a network of traders, usually linked by fancy technology, who transfer the ownership of the various commodities using contracts for the underlying goods. This form of organization makes it possible for buyers, sellers, hedgers, and speculators to trade commodities without a physical exchange of the goods taking place. But that's not all.

The contracts themselves can be for immediate delivery (the spot market) or for delivery in the future (the futures market), although hedgers and speculators generally close out their side of the contract before it expires and delivery falls due.

Commodity exchanges are an excellent refinement in markets. Consider the logistical (and financial) problem faced by a buyer who needs to purchase an enormous quantity of coconut oil. Absent a commodity exchange, she might have to travel the world, taking whatever price obtains when she arrives at any particular market place. Ditto for a seller whose coconut oil might turn rancid while he waits dockside for a buyer to show up. Commodity exchanges also permit buyers and sellers to hedge existing positions. If the price of coconut oil is low, the coconut oil buyer, for instance, might buy a futures contract to hedge against the possibility that prices will rise before she makes her purchase. And if the price is high, the seller might sell futures contracts to hedge against the possibility that prices will fall before he makes his sale.

There are dozens and dozens of commodities which are traded on an exchange, among them wheat, corn, cotton, cocoa, sugar, coffee, soybeans, pork, beef, frozen orange juice, rubber, gold, silver, copper, fur, and lumber. There are also some exotica traded that are not raw materials but financial instruments (foreign currencies, U.S. Treasuries, and stock indexes). *See* FUTURES MARKET; SPOT MARKET.

COMMON STOCK

Shares in the equity capital of a corporation that give holders a claim to the assets of the corporation.

That definition is correct, but it leaves out some vital information. First, in the case of financial trouble, common stock holders' claims to the corporation's assets can be gratified only after the bond holders, preferred stock holders, debenture holders, other creditors, and the IRS have been satisfied. And second, although there's a lot of blather about how common stock holders are owners of the corporation and have a say in management, that's true only for stockholders who have equal voting rights—not all do.

Generally investors buy common stock either because they are optimistic that the firm will be wildly profitable and they will be able to sell their shares later for lots more money than they paid for them, or because they are optimistic that the firm will be modestly profitable and they will receive reasonable and predictable dividends. In either case, common stock holders take the risk that the firm will do neither and they will lose their money.

CONGLOMERATE

A huge corporation consisting of many different types of businesses. It's not unusual, for instance, to have a conglomerate that bakes bread, runs hotels, flies airplanes, oversees a telecommunications business, and sells insurance.

A conglomerate is the result of a series of mergers or takeovers, usually undertaken by a firm wishing to diversify its risk —that is, if profits slip in one market, the conglomerate can still count on profits from businesses operating in other markets.

CONSUMER PRICE INDEX

Monthly measure that tracks changes in price levels. Also known as the CPI, this is usually what people are referring to when they talk about the cost of living going up or down.

The CPI itself is made up of 100,000 prices—everything from the cost of housing to apples and oranges. Prices are gathered once a month by the federal government and weighted to reflect a typical family's budget. Housing, for example, constitutes 43 percent of this (playfully named) "market basket" of goods and services.

The CPI is one of the most intensely watched economic indicators. And for good reason. A lot depends on its every wiggle.

For one thing, changes in the CPI determine the size of payments under all sorts of contracts from labor, royalty, and divorce agreements to Social Security checks. A small bounce up can trigger the payout of billions of extra bucks.

For another thing, changes in the CPI determine how investors manage their money. For example, when the CPI starts showing sustained monthly increases, investors will become anxious that the economy is in for a period of inflation and will begin to adjust their portfolios. Usually that means they will shift out of financial assets like stocks and bonds in favor of "inflation-proof" assets like gold, real estate, and collectibles. (Expect to see the reverse investment strategy, of course, if the CPI starts showing monthly declines.)

CONVERTIBLE

(Informally known as a convert.) Something that can be exchanged for something else, like a preferred stock or bond which can be traded for a common stock.

That definition is correct but admittedly pretty fuzzy. So here is a more precise one: A security (like a debenture) issued by a corporation which promises that the holder can convert it into another type of security (like common stock) within a specified amount of time at a specified price and a specified ratio (one convertible bond equals so many shares of common stock).

Investors like convertibles because, in their first state as a bond or preferred stock, they are less risky than common stock, and in their converted state as common stock, they allow investors to share in future capital gains. In other words, investors prefer convertibles when they are feeling optimistic about a company's prospects, but aren't totally convinced—a convert protects more of their original investment. If they become more convinced that the company will prove out, they can then convert into common stock.

Companies like convertibles because interest costs are lower in the converts' first state as a bond or preferred stock (they cost less than regular debt), and, as holders convert them into common stock, company balance sheets will show less debt and more equity.

CORPORATION

A legal entity or business organization in which the owners enjoy something called limited liability.

Enjoy? Sure. The corporation can be sued but not the stockholders, and, if the corporation goes bankrupt, only its assets —not the personal assets of its stockholders—can be used to liquidate its debt. (In the case of bankruptcy, of course, the stockholders of the corporation could lose the entire value of their stake.)

The corporate form is a very effective way to raise large amounts of capital. And the fact that it is an independent legal entity means that if—worst case—any of its stockholders or management dies, the corporation can keep on doing business with new stockholders or management. The drawback to this form of organization is that because corporations tend to be giant enterprises, with ownership scattered among thousands of stockholders, the real control rests with management, who may have their own best interests at heart and not that of the owners.

CREDIT

The mechanism that allows goods or services to be sold on the promise of future payment.

Credit is a fact of life. Business uses credit to finance everyday matters (like inventories) and occasional undertakings (like plant expansions). And consumers use credit to finance spur-of-the-moment purchases (baubles) and thought-out ones (cars and houses).

And it's no exaggeration to say that credit is a desirable fact of life. A credit economy functions with greater smoothness and at a higher level than a strictly cash economy. First, credit is more convenient than money for big purchases. Without credit, businesses would have to employ fleets of armored cars to ferry their cash to suppliers or to the bank. Ditto for consumers: Without credit, shopping sprees would be incredibly burdensome. To put it in economists' lingo: Credit allows people to economize on their use of money.

Second, credit facilitates a multitude of activities by allowing people to have the use of things before they actually own them. Installment credit, for example, lets a homemaker pay for the services of a washer-dryer as he uses it.

Business credit varies in form from "book" credit (it's carried as an entry on the seller's books) to written forms like letters of credit, trade acceptances, and promissory notes; consumer credit comes in the form of charge accounts, credit cards, installment credit, and consumer loans.

CREDIT CRUNCH

A situation in which people want more credit than the economy can easily make available.

Credit crunches usually happen after the economy has been growing at a rapid clip; that is, after a period during which business has borrowed a lot of money to expand its operations and consumers have taken on a lot of debt to finance their purchases. This strong demand for credit draws down the pool of credit (the savings made available to spenders), leaving would-be spenders to battle over the remaining funds. The crunch itself comes when their battle drives up interest rates (the price of credit). This type of credit crunch is considered a normal stage in the business cycle.

Credit crunches can also be manufactured by the Federal Reserve Board. The Fed can either suddenly restrict the supply of money in the economy or raise the amount of money its member banks must reserve against their deposits, thus contracting the supply of credit. Typically, the Fed engineers a credit crunch to cool off an overheated economy, a situation which it fears will either lead to, or has already caused, high rates of inflation.

In either case, when the credit crunch drives interest rates high enough, businesses and consumers cut back on their spending, thus sending the economy into the contractionary phase of the business cycle.

CYCLICAL STOCK

Common stock in an industry group which is thought to be very responsive to the ups and downs of the business cycle. In other words, when economic activity is slack, cyclical stocks will lose a lot of value, and when economic activity perks up, these stocks will gain a lot of value. Cyclical stocks are thus more risky than, say, defensive stocks. Industries which are considered very cyclical are commodities like copper and paper. *See* DEFENSIVE STOCK; GROWTH STOCK; INTEREST RATE SENSITIVE STOCK.

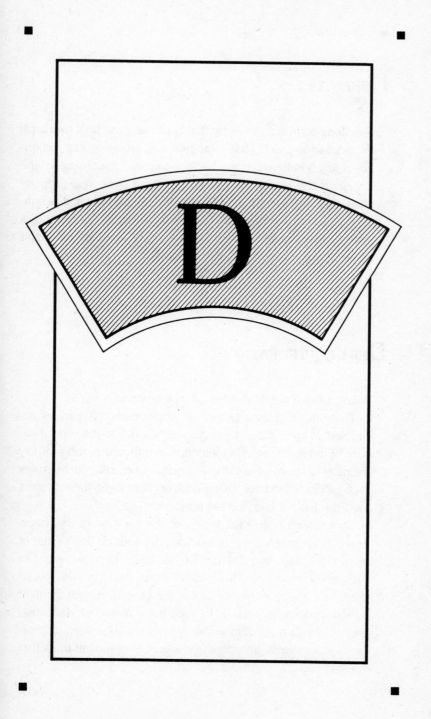

DEBENTURE

Any long-term debt security that is not secured by a mortgage on a specific asset. That's another way of saying that debentures are bonds which are backed only by the earnings of the issuer. If the issuer goes bankrupt, there is no real property the debenture holder can lay claim to. (A subordinated debenture is a debt security with even less status. In the event of a bankruptcy, holders of subordinated debt are paid only after other, more senior, creditors are satisfied.)

DEBT-EQUITY RATIO

A firm's funded debt divided by its total equity.

This ratio is a favorite tool for stock analysts. When it's expressed in percentage terms, it yields a quick-and-dirty measure of indebtedness: If indebtedness in the framistan industry averages 30 percent and the Framistan Company's debt-equity ratio is $5 million over $10 million, or 50 percent, then chances are Framistan is carrying too much debt.

That having been said, however, the question of whether a firm has too much debt, or too little, depends on one's point of view. Debt financing, or financial leverage, can go two ways. In bad times, of course, the cost of fixed debt (interest costs) might rise above the firm's profits, forcing it to service the debt by reducing equity's share. In good times, however, debt costs might fall below the firm's return on assets, thus swelling profits. In other words, investors who like leverage might think that

Framistan's 50 percent is just right—or perhaps too low. *See* FINANCIAL RATIOS; LEVERAGE.

DEFAULT

In general, the failure to fulfill an obligation; specifically, the failure to pay the interest or principal on debt obligations when those payments fall due. After this failure takes place, the offending debtor is said to be "in default." (Being in default is grim, but it's not as serious as being bankrupt or—worst case —being defunct.)

DEFENSIVE STOCK

Common stock in an industry group which is thought to be relatively immune to the ups and downs of the business cycle. In other words, defensive stocks won't lose a lot of value in periods of slack economic activity, nor will they gain a lot of value when economic growth is gangbusters. Defensive stocks are less risky than, say, cyclical stocks. Industries and/or stock groups considered to be defensive are food and drugs. *See* CYCLICAL STOCK; GROWTH STOCK; INTEREST RATE SENSITIVE STOCK.

DEFLATION

A situation of generally falling prices. Deflation, like all big economic events, can be caused by many things. Usually, however, it's the result of high interest rates which have forced business and consumers to cut back on spending.

As an idea, deflation doesn't sound like a bad thing, especially if it follows a period of wicked inflation. Indeed, the very event of falling prices should call forth its own solution: Lower prices should encourage people to start spending again and prices should rise. The problem is, that only holds true in theory. In reality, deflation can be quite unpleasant.

Not all prices fall during a period of deflation. Some prices, such as farm prices, are maintained by the government, and some, as with labor contracts, are set by long-term agreement. Consider what happens during real-life deflation.

When high interest rates cause a drop in spending, some businesses will be left with unsold goods. Now, if those firms cannot lower their prices because they are constrained by labor contracts—that is, if they cut prices, they will not be able to cover their labor costs—then these firms will cut back on their output. Of course, if they produce less, they will need fewer workers. So one result of deflation is unemployment. And unemployment means even less spending as people are laid off.

As for the firms that do lower prices, they will earn less and quite probably spend less on things like capital improvements. Again, deflation will result in even less spending.

Thus, if prices cannot fall, people will be unemployed, and if prices do fall, people will earn less. Either way, spending will drop and the economy will languish.

Don't confuse deflation with disinflation. Unlike deflation, disinflation is generally good: It means that prices are not increasing as fast as they were, or that inflation is slowing down. *See* DISINFLATION; INFLATION.

DEPRECIATION (ASSETS)

Term used to describe the process in which an asset loses its value.

Here's the straightforward part. Companies use various kinds of assets, like machinery, to produce things. And the wear and tear involved in using those assets erodes their value. Thus, in order to get a clear idea of how much a company's fixed assets are worth, this wear and tear must be accounted for. Accordingly, each year the company writes down some part of its assets' original value.

Now, here's the less straightforward part. Just how an asset is depreciated depends on a number of things: how much it cost when new, how long it is expected to remain useful, and what, if any, salvage value it is expected to have. Note that two of those things involve estimates. And once those questions are answered, the actual calculation of depreciation depends on what formula is used.

In the straight line method, the cost of the asset, minus its salvage value, is simply divided by the number of years the asset will be used, resulting in an annual depreciation expense which is constant. Other methods, however, produce variable annual expense figures: The sum-of-the-digits method, for example, results in a greater depreciation expense in the early years than in the later years.

This kind of flexibility in accounting for depreciation is more than a green eyeshade trick. Since profits are calculated after depreciation costs are netted out, companies can choose the depreciation method which will give them the most favorable tax liability. For instance, a company using a depreciation schedule which yields a bigger expense in the near term will also pay less taxes in the near term.

DEPRECIATION (CURRENCY)

A fall in the price of a currency relative to other currencies.

Under a system of floating exchange rates, the market sets the value of currencies. A nation with a "weak" currency—one that other nations don't want to own—will see its currency decline in value relative to other currencies. The nation with the depreciating currency will usually find itself eventually with a trade surplus as its export goods become cheaper and its imports become more expensive. Politically, nations like to run trade surpluses, so it's more difficult to get them to officially appreciate their currency. *See* APPRECIATION (CURRENCY); FOREIGN EXCHANGE.

DEPRESSION

When economic growth turns steeply negative for a prolonged period. During the Great Depression of the 1930s, for example, employment, production, prices, wages, interest rates, and profits zoomed down and stayed low.

In business cycle jargon, depressions are just like recessions, only more so. (A recession is defined as any period in which the gross national product falls for at least two quarters.) However, since the political party in power prefers to call even a serious downturn in the business cycle a recession, "depression" has become a term used by the party not in power.

DEVALUATION

Lowering the value of a nation's currency under fixed exchange rates.

A fixed exchange rate arises when governments declare that their currencies will have a fixed value in relation to other currencies or to gold. Devaluation, then, must come about as a deliberate action on the part of government.

Say, for example, $35 in U.S. currency buys one ounce of gold. Now, if the United States wants to devalue, it will raise the price of gold by declaring that henceforth it will take more dollars to buy one ounce of gold. If the United States raises the price of gold to $38, then it has also lowered the value of the dollar by 7.9 percent. That is, it now takes 7.9 percent more dollars to buy one ounce of gold. If other nations maintain the price of gold in their own currencies, then the value of the dollar will have fallen relative to those currencies. Simply put, it will also take more dollars to buy French francs or German marks.

Devaluation is usually undertaken when a nation is running a troublesome trade deficit with other nations. By decreasing the value of its currency and thus increasing the value of other currencies, the devaluing nation makes it cheaper for other nations to buy its goods and more expensive for its citizens to buy foreign goods. Hence, exports from the devaluing nation will go up, imports will go down, and the trade deficit should disappear.

The United States went off a fixed exchange rate in 1971, allowing the dollar to float up or down as the foreign exchange market dictates. *See* DEPRECIATION (CURRENCY).

DISCOUNT HOUSE

A brokerage firm that buys and sells stocks, and often other financial instruments, for its clients at cut-rate prices.

Discount houses, as opposed to full service brokerage firms, can charge less money for transactions because they only execute orders. Instead of a full service broker, who will phone you with ideas and send you masses of financial literature, a discount house employs plain old clerks who just answer the phone and do what you tell them to do. (The nice thing about a discount house is that it's cheap and it doesn't deluge you with all sorts of advice and products. The drawback is that if you want to do some harebrained trade, nobody will try to dissuade you.)

DISCOUNTING

Strictly speaking, discounting is the process of finding the present value of a series of future cash flows.

Less strictly speaking, discounting is a way of evaluating

investments by taking the time value of money into consideration. How? Simple. Say the interest rate is 10 percent. A year from now you would earn $10 on an investment of $100. Thus, the present value of $110 a year from now is $100 today; similarly, $121 two years from now and $133 three years from now are worth $100 today. (Or, said more gracefully, $100 invested today at 10 percent a year will yield $110 after one year, $121 after two years, and $133 after three years.) Consider, then, two ways in which discounting is actually used. This isn't quite so simple.

The first is called net present value. It is a calculation which gathers together the future value of an investment and recasts it in today's dollars. The interest rate is called the discount rate because it is used to discount the expected cash flow from the investment over time. (Exactly as in the example above, $110 a year from now, discounted at 10 percent, will yield the $100 investment.) In this case, discounting will yield the present value of the investment after the cost of the investment, the discount rate, and the cash flow are plugged into the formula. In other words, net present value tells investors how much the investment over time is worth in today's dollars.

The second way of discounting is by finding the internal rate of return. Here the formula estimates the rate of return earned by the project after the cost of the investment and its expected stream of revenues are plugged in. Calculating the internal rate of return will tell investors what rate of return they can expect to earn on the investment.

Thus, using one of these two formulas to discount various investment projects helps investors decide which are likely to yield the highest returns.

There is another, much more informal, use of the word "discounting." When new information prompts investors to buy or sell a stock and thus change its price, people on Wall Street are fond of saying that the information has been discounted in the price; they mean that the new price reflects the new— loosely put—wisdom.

DISCOUNTING THE NEWS, *or* DISCOUNTED IN THE PRICE

Standard Wall Street reason for why the price of something doesn't budge after something is announced which was expected to move the price.

This is one of those entries which is better explained by an example. Say the stock market has been in a blah period and that Wall Street types have been saying that all the market needs is some economic good news to send it skyrocketing. And then say that some really dynamite development in the economy becomes public knowledge. If the market then fails to respond by surging up, the same Wall Street types will now say that the good news was "already discounted" by the market. They mean that somehow the market had anticipated and already incorporated this good news.

This handy little notion is often used by brokers who had been assuring clients that once some piece of news or some development was announced, the price of whatever stock they were touting would sail ever upwards. If the price doesn't change, however, the broker will say the news was "already discounted in the price." Listener, beware.

DISINFLATION

A slowing in the rate of inflation. Granted, that sounds disingenuous, but it's not. Say prices rise 7 percent a year for several years, putting inflation at 7 percent. If the price rise suddenly drops to 4 percent a year, then—even though prices are still going in an inflationary direction—the decline in the rate is disinflationary. Don't confuse disinflation with deflation, where prices actually go down. *See* DEFLATION; INFLATION.

DIVERSIFICATION

Reducing risk by not putting all one's eggs in one basket. A company, for example, might diversify by making more than one product or by buying other companies which produce different products. That way, if sales of one product line slump, strong sales of other products can maintain the company's earnings.

Investors, too, can diversify. They might, for instance, buy stock in a diversified company. But usually investors reduce their risk by holding diverse investments (this is called, unsurprisingly, portfolio diversification). They might buy stock in a mutual fund which owns lots of different companies, buy both domestic and foreign stocks, or buy different kinds of assets, like stocks, bonds, and commodities.

Dividend

Payment to stockholder as his or her share of profits.

Dividends are declared by the corporation's board of directors; they are usually paid quarterly and in cash. The amount of the dividend due to preferred stockholders is a fixed amount, while the amount due to common stockholders is supposed to vary with profits. (Supposed to. Most corporations prefer to keep dividend payments constant, even when profits dip.) *See* EX-DIVIDEND.

Dow-Jones Averages

Three groups of stock prices—thirty industrial companies, twenty transportation companies, and fifteen utilities—reported as three measures of market activity and recorded daily in terms of their highs, lows, and closing prices.

The best known of the three is the Dow-Jones Industrial Average. Indeed, it's the index that people have in mind when they talk about how the stock market is doing; phrases like "The Dow is up ten points" or "The Dow is falling" refer to the DJIA.

Although the Dow has become popularly synonymous with the stock market, professionals refer to—and watch—another measure, the Standard & Poor's 500 index because it's more representative of the stock market. *See* STANDARD & POOR'S 500 COMPOSITE INDEX.

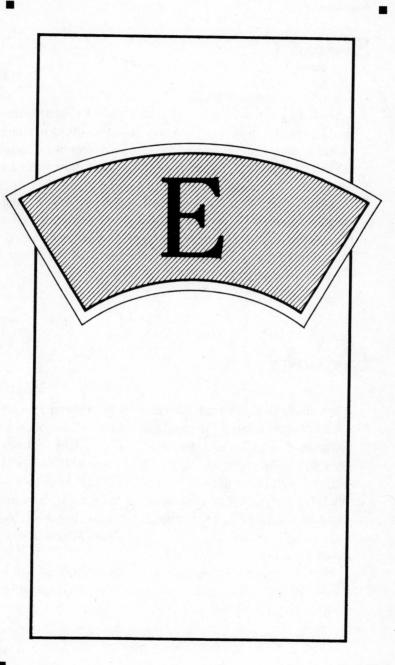

EARNINGS

A firm's net income, or profit.

Some of a firm's income can be set aside for internal use (like buying new machinery), in which case it's called retained earnings; and some of its income can be given out to stockholders as dividends, in which case it's called distributed income.

A firm's earnings also figure in an important financial ratio called earnings per share. Here, earnings are what's left after taxes, depreciation, interest, and other expenses are deducted. That number is then divided by the number of shares of common stock outstanding.

EASY MONEY

A seemingly blissful situation created by the Federal Reserve Bank to reduce interest rates and expand the amount of credit available. Blissful because the combination of lower interest rates and more credit means that borrowers who had been shut out of the debt market can now go in to borrow money "cheaply." Seemingly blissful because the long-term result might be that money lent for dubious projects cannot be paid back when easy money becomes tight again. Which is what always happens.

When money is easy, investors usually favor financial instruments like stocks, because abundant credit is usually good for companies. But if easy money creates too much inflation, investors will usually turn to hard assets like real estate and commodities, because their prices usually rise faster than the rate of inflation. *See* TIGHT MONEY.

EFFECTIVE RATE OF INTEREST

See BOND YIELD.

EFFICIENT MARKET HYPOTHESIS

Financial theory which holds that information is rapidly disseminated and reflected in stock prices so that the market price of a security equals its investment value at all times.

This theory, like many others, rests on some rather fantastic assumptions: that all investors have equal access not only to good information, but to information about the future, that all investors are smart enough to interpret the information correctly, and that all investors quickly move to buy and/or sell securities based on the information.

These pie-in-the-skyish assumptions should render this theory harmless. Should. Nonetheless, it is viewed with alarm by Wall Street professionals. After all, if the market price of a stock is always an accurate reflection of its investment value, then who needs a herd of brokers and analysts? Or, more to the point, who would believe their claims to have ferreted out a "little-known, cheap" stock? *See* RANDOM WALK HYPOTHESIS.

EQUITY

Properly speaking, the value of a firm minus its liabilities. Less properly, another name for stock. (The less correct definition comes from something called equity capital, which refers to the investment in a company by its owners. Equity capital is supplied by investors who buy new shares in a company— hence the phrase "they're raising equity capital," which means a company is selling stock.)

EURODOLLARS

Dollars held outside the United States. Generally, Eurodollars take the form of large, short-term loans on deposits made in dollars at banks outside the United States. (Just like domestic bank lending, the Eurodollar market is a way of creating and using credit.)

Dollars can escape the domestic banking system in several ways. Essentially, though, they find their way to other countries as the result of international trade. Let's say you buy a bucket of Arabian oil and pay for it with a dollar-denominated check drawn on your bank. The seller then deposits those dollars in his own bank or, more likely, in a London bank or a London branch of an American bank. Voilà—dollars which can be lent outside of the U.S.: Eurodollars.

Perhaps the main reason for these expatriate dollars is that reserve requirements and other regulations are less severe abroad than in the United States. Thus, interest rates on Eurodollar deposits are often higher than U.S. rates and borrowers often pay lower interest rates for Eurodollar credit.

Dollars were the first currency to become Euroized; now, however, there is Eurocurrency—Euroyen, Eurosterling and so on. Indeed, the Euromarket goes beyond Euroland into Asia, the Caribbean, and so on and encompasses Eurobonds, or bonds denominated in Euroyen, Eurodollars, and so on. Anyway, not to belabor the point, Euroization is part of the globalization of the world's economy.

Ex-DIVIDEND

Literally, a sale of stock in which the dividend is excluded.

Dividend excluded? How could that happen? Well, if a corporation's board of directors declares a dividend for the shareholders of record on a certain date and an owner sells his or her shares after that date but before the actual dividend is paid, then the buyer has bought the shares ex-dividend—the payment goes to the shareholder as of the record date.

FACE VALUE

Nominal, or stated, value, as opposed to market value.

The face value of a bond, for example, is the amount that is printed on it. Ditto for the face value of a postage stamp or a coin. Nonetheless, formality aside, the market value of the bond or stamp or coin might differ markedly from its face value. Buyers might be willing to pay much more than face value if the bond carries an above-market interest rate, if the stamp is a rare one, or if the coin is made of gold. (Of course, that goes either way: The market value could also be less than the face value.) *See* PAR VALUE.

FANNIE MAE, FEDERAL NATIONAL MORTGAGE ASSOCIATION

A private corporation which purchases real estate mortgages. Fannie Mae raises funds by issuing its own bonds and notes, and its stock sells on the New York Stock Exchange. *See* GINNIE MAE.

THE FED

Nickname for both the Federal Reserve System and its most visible part, the Federal Reserve Board. The Fed is our central bank, the bank of banks; its clients are commercial banks and the government.

The Fed was created in 1913. It consists of twelve banks spread across the country and a board of governors located in Washington. All the interesting action, however, takes place in Washington, where seven governors and the chairperson direct the half-dozen functions that make the Fed a very heavy hitter in determining the course of the economy and what's loosely called the investment climate.

The Fed's most important function is to control the money supply. This is accomplished through two activities: buying and selling government securities and changing reserve requirements. The key to understanding these activities is knowing how the Fed interacts with its member banks. Once this relationship is understood, everything else will fall into place.

Banks are required to keep reserves against the money they loan. If you open an account at a bank by depositing $1,000, the bank cannot turn around and lend out the entire $1,000; it must reserve some fraction of that amount. Banks which are members of the Federal Reserve—that includes most banks and all big ones—are required to keep a minimum amount of reserves against their deposits. These reserves are usually held as deposits in the Federal Reserve System. It is through its grip on these bank reserves that the Fed is able to keep its hand on the loan activities of banks and thus on the economy.

Now back to just how the Fed controls the money supply. The Fed's most powerful activity, the buying and selling of government bonds, is carried on by something called the Federal Open Market Committee, which does something called open-market operations. Say the Fed thinks the economy is overheating—business is expanding too fast and/or inflation is rising too steeply. The Federal Open Market Committee will then move to restrict the amount of credit available. It will sell government securities.

The buyers of these securities pay the Fed with checks written on their banks. When the Fed presents these checks to the banks, they pay out of their reserves. Thus, the banks end up with both less reserves and less money on deposit. With less money available, of course, the banks have to cut back on the amount of loans they can make or their reserves will fall below the minimum requirement. And when banks restrict loan (or credit) activity, the economy slows down.

The second, but less used, device to control the amount of credit in the economy is the Fed's power to set reserve requirements. Again, say that the Fed wishes to slow credit activity. In this case, all it has to do is increase the amount of reserves it requires its member banks to keep on hand. Thus, with a larger fraction of deposits going into reserve accounts, banks will have less to lend.

A third, and also critical, function of the Fed is to act as the lender of last resort. This activity is accomplished through what's called the Fed's discount window. (The discount window is the fanciful name given to the Fed's own lending activities.) When member banks are short of cash, they can borrow money from the Fed for a fee, known as the discount rate. When the Fed wants to encourage bank credit activity, it lowers the discount rate, making it cheaper for banks to borrow. When the Fed wants to restrict activity, it raises the discount rate, making it more expensive.

Lending as a last resort is required when some event causes financial panic. Say that a big bank gets stuck with a lot of bad loans. Once the word gets out that the bank is having "difficulty," depositors might panic, another fanciful term meaning they will start to demand their money. If enough depositors call for their money, the bank will have to close its doors. (Yet another fanciful term meaning that the bank has run out of ready cash with which to back, or refund, deposits.)

Of course, a bank with closed doors means that no depositor can cash in his or her account, and that people will stop accepting checks drawn on the closed bank. If the panic gets out of hand, depositors at otherwise sound banks will suddenly start demanding their money. Then banks will have to use their reserves and, when their reserves run out, start calling in their loans or shutting their own doors. In other words, the banking system will be faced with a first-class liquidity crisis.

But the Fed, by making cash available to the banks, can stop the panic. Simply put, when the Fed motors out cash through its discount window, anxious depositors realize that the Fed stands ready to ensure that they can have their cash whenever they want it. Thus, depositors will be less likely to all show up at the same time demanding money, and banks can go on about their business of taking deposits and making loans.

One of the more controversial functions of the Fed, especially in the past few years, has been its role in financing government budget deficits. When the government spends more than it collects in taxes, it covers the difference by borrowing from the public. That is, the Treasury issues debt securities in the form of notes, bills, and bonds. More colorfully put, the Treasury prints some money.

If the Fed decides to go along with the Treasury, it will buy those debt securities, thus injecting money into the financial system. How? By just the opposite process of what happens when the Fed sells government securities, as described above. When the Fed pays for its purchases, it increases the reserves held by its member banks. And with more reserves on hand, the banks suddenly have more money to lend. This process is called monetizing the debt, and it usually leads to inflation.

Net-net, then, the Fed is an extremely powerful institution.

It controls the nation's money supply and thus is an important player in determining whether credit is easy or tight, whether prices go up or down, and whether times are good or lousy. For instance, the Fed refused to act as the lender of last resort during the Great Depression and thereby prolonged it; it pumped out too much money in the 1970s and thereby contributed to double-digit inflation; and it clamped down sharply in the early 1980s and thereby caused a nasty recession. In fact, some economists—and a lot of journalists—call the chairperson of the Fed the second most powerful person in the country. That, of course, is the kind of silly oversimplification that gives both economics and journalism a bad name.

Nonetheless, the Fed's impact on the course of the economy makes it one of those things that are followed closely by investors. There is, in fact, an entire industry of so-called Fed watchers who claim to interpret its every breath to a ready audience.

These Fed watchers, many of whom are employed by Wall Street firms, inspect the data on the money supply and the public utterances of the Fed's main players. They then try to predict both what the Fed is going to do—whether it is going to expand or contract credit—and how that action will affect the investment climate. Occasionally, some Fed watchers become almost as powerful as the Fed itself, and their predictions move the market. If, for example, a famous Fed watcher declares that interest rates are going to go down, he might cause investors to buy bonds and sell stocks. But this power obtains only in the short term. In the long term, the power of any Fed watcher is only as sound as his or her predictions because it is actual Fed policy which affects the economy and thus moves the market. *See* BANKS AND BANKING.

■ FINANCIAL RATIOS

Finance

A verb that means to provide money, as in "How are you going to finance that deal?"

Consumers can finance purchases through various types of borrowing—installment credit, credit card credit, or mortgages. Firms can finance, or raise money, by issuing stocks, bonds, or notes; by borrowing from a bank; or by keeping some of their earnings.

Financial intermediary

An institution which links savers with borrowers. Financial intermediaries include banks, savings and loan associations, finance companies, insurance companies, and pension plans.

The process of financial intermediation is simple. Savers are those who wish to put their own money to work—that is, they want to earn money with their money. Borrowers are those who wish to put other people's money to work. Financial intermediaries stand between these two groups as middlemen and offer savers a fee for lending money and charge borrowers a fee for using it.

Financial ratios

Various types of measures used to gauge the financial or economic health of a firm. (They can also be used for figuring

87 ■

whether the stock market is about to go up or down and other such fortune-tellerish topics.)

Ratios are a favorite tool of stock analysts and other Wall Street types who use them to figure out why some companies are or will be better than others. There are, in fact, over two dozen ratios that are universally and regularly pressed into service and countless others that have been tailored to serve individual purposes.

Ratios are handy little devices because they permit apples to be measured against oranges—for example, by reducing a company's specific numbers to a general relationship, companies of differing sizes can be compared. Nonetheless, as with all mechanical devices, it's hard to evaluate the results. Company A may have a higher debt-equity ratio than Company B, but that doesn't mean that Company B is in better financial condition. Nor does it mean that Company B's future prospects are brighter.

Among the most commonly used are the current ratio (total current assets divided by total current liabilities), the acid-test or quick ratio (relatively liquid assets divided by total current liabilities), and the inventory turnover ratio (cost of goods sold divided by average inventory). *See* DEBT-EQUITY RATIO; PRICE-EARNINGS RATIO.

FINANCIAL STATEMENTS

Accounting statements supposedly designed to give a good look at a firm's financial position and operations.

Financial statements are what follow the glossy photos in a firm's annual report. They usually consist of a balance sheet, an income statement, a statement of retained earnings, and a statement of changes in financial position.

The numbers which appear on the various financial statements are supposed to be collected and displayed according to generally accepted accounting principles, or GAAP. And the auditor's report, which comes at the end of the financial statements, is supposed to certify that these principles have been followed. This is all supposed to mean that users of the financial statements can be confident that nobody has "cooked the books"; what it really means is that if somebody has misrepresented the firm's financial position, it was done too cleverly to be detected. (For a while, anyway.) *See* ANNUAL REPORT; BALANCE SHEET; INCOME STATEMENT.

FIRM

A business unit which produces goods or services. A firm hires labor, buys material, engages space (and perhaps borrows some money), and then combines those factors of production to make something that it can sell. Firms hope to earn profits by their activities.

Consider a firm like a pizzeria. To produce pizza, the owner of the firm might rent a place of business, install various equipment like an oven (and a cash register), hire a pizza maker, buy the ingredients for dough and sauce (along with cheese, sausage, and whatever), and then organize all the above to produce pizza. The point, of course, is that the firm can then sell the output—pizza—for more money than it needs to pay for all the inputs.

Ownership of firms can range from a single individual to

millions of stockholders. A group of firms all in the same business constitutes an industry.

FLOAT

A noun referring to a gap between the time a check is written and the time it appears as a credit to a bank account.

A float can be either good or bad depending on what side of the transaction you are on. If you are the check writer, then the float is in your favor until it is debited to your account. If you are the recipient, however, the float is against you until the deposited check is credited to your account. (The joke line "The check is in the mail" is a good reflection of how frustrating it is to be on the wrong side of the float.)

("Float" can also refer to something more specialized—the amount of a new security that has been issued but not yet been bought by the public.)

FOREIGN EXCHANGE, FOREIGN EXCHANGE MARKET, EXCHANGE RATE

The first two terms are a snap to define. Foreign exchange refers to claims to hard cash in the currencies of foreign countries. The foreign exchange market is where foreign exchange is traded; it's an international marketplace whose players, connected by telephones and computers, arrange for the transfer of currencies from one country or person to another. Trading can take place either immediately (the spot market) or in the future (the forward market).

But the third term, exchange rate, is not so easy. Quickly defined, an exchange rate is the price at which one currency can be traded for another. But that definition raises two questions: Why are exchange rates necessary, and how are they determined?

Exchange rates are necessary because countries engage in foreign trade. When buyers and sellers exchange goods, they each want to make the transaction in their own currency. Simple enough.

But trade is an uneven process. Countries have different fiscal and monetary policies, so they have different growth rates, interest rates, and inflationary expectations. Countries also have different cost structures, so that prices of identical goods may vary from country to country. Too, some countries may make unique products. All these differences mean that some countries have so-called strong currencies—ones in great demand—while others have weak currencies—ones for which demand is slight. Thus, currencies have different relative values, and trading partners need a mechanism which converts the value of one currency into the currency of another.

Consider what happens when Americans buy French wine. Americans wish to trade their dollars for wine, but the French wish to trade their wine for francs. So dollars must be exchanged for francs if the trade is to go forward.

The exchange rate indicates how many francs—and thus how much wine—a dollar will buy. The exchange rate between dollars and francs gives the American buyer and the French seller the chance to evaluate the trade in terms of their own currencies. If the exchange rate is nine francs to one dollar, then $100 will purchase 900 francs' worth of wine in France.

And now for the second question: How are exchange rates determined? Here the answer depends on what kind of exchange rate system countries choose to operate under. There are more or less three choices: a fixed rate, a floating rate, or a managed rate.

Under a fixed rate system, countries agree on a set, or "par," value for their currencies. For example, the exchange rate between German marks and American dollars could be set at three marks to one dollar, or the exchange rate between French francs and American dollars could be set at nine to one.

The central banks of each country must then agree to hold reserves of all currencies and to buy and sell from these reserves to offset deviations from par values. If, for example, an excellent vintage of French wine causes a rush of wine buyers in other countries to demand francs, the value of the franc might rise above its par value. In that case, the French central bank must sell francs and buy other currencies in order to restore equilibrium.

Under a floating rate system, on the other hand, the market sets the value of currencies based on supply and demand. Say the demand for dollars is great because of high interest rates, good investment possibilities, low inflationary expectations, or a fierce desire to buy American goods and services. Then the dollar's exchange rate will be high. A floating rate system means that exchange rates are flexible and free to change from hour to hour or minute to minute.

Needless to say, a floating rate regime means that central banks cannot intervene in the market to adjust the price of currencies. For example, if a great vintage causes heavy demand for francs, the central bank of France is supposed to just watch as the franc appreciates against other currencies.

Under a managed float, the third type of exchange rate regime, countries say they are on a floating rate system but act as if they were under a fixed rate one. That is, central banks allow the market to set the exchange rate—unless they disagree with the result. The net of a managed float, also called a dirty float, is that currencies appreciate and depreciate only as much as central banks permit.

During the 1950s and 1960s, most major currencies were on a fixed, but periodically adjustable, regime. At present most major currencies are on a floating but managed system. Neither of those regimes seems to work very well, so the debate over how an international monetary system should be run is still a hot one. And an important one.

There are several arguments against floating exchange rates. Most dramatically, when the foreign exchange price of a currency goes up and down, trading relationships are disturbed and the domestic economy suffers. Say the dollar depreciates against the currencies of our trading partners. While that makes our exports cheap, it also makes foreign imports expensive. Eventually, as the demand for foreign imports shrinks, business and jobs in the import sector will be lost.

Too, floating rates can be inflationary. In terms of a depreciating dollar, for instance, the rise in the dollar price of imports both provides a shield for domestic industries to raise their prices and pushes up costs for industries dependent on imported materials.

Furthermore, without the discipline imposed on central banks to keep their currencies at an agreed-upon value, central banks can—and do—pursue inflationary increases in the money supply. (Under a fixed rate system, if banks create too much money, their currency starts to depreciate and they are then bound to start buying their own currency—thereby reducing the supply—in order to restore exchange rate equilibrium.)

There are also, of course, several arguments against fixed exchange rates. To begin with, the requirement that governments keep their currencies stable can create distortions in trade. A country faced with a depreciating currency might not wish to undergo the often painful measures needed to bring its currency back into line. Instead, the government might try to restrict imports by passing protectionist laws.

So, too, central banks can always weasel around the discipline of the fixed rate system. Say a dollar depreciation causes the Fed to go out and buy up dollars abroad; the Fed can then turn around and put those dollars back into domestic circulation by buying bonds.

Floating exchange rates also offer opportunities for investment—or speculation. Indeed, there are a lot of people all over the world who trade foreign currencies just as other investors trade stocks and bonds. These traders will buy a lot of a currency they expect to appreciate in value or dump a lot of a currency they expect to depreciate in value.

Too, floating exchange rates make it prudent for more regular types to plan ahead. Say that you're going to vacation in France in a few months; you think that the franc is low relative to the value of the dollar but are nervous that this favorable relationship will reverse itself by the time your plane touches down in Paris. Prudence requires that you buy a bunch of francs now. Ditto for businesspeople who expect to have to pay for foreign goods in the future. If the exchange rate looks good in the present, they buy whatever foreign currency they'll need in the future. *See* FORWARD MARKET; GOLD STANDARD.

FORWARD MARKET

Although this term can refer to any futures market where promises to buy or sell something at a future date are made and traded, it usually refers to the futures market in foreign currencies.

This will go better with an example of how a transaction in the forward exchange market might work. Say an American businesswoman sells a bunch of framistans to a French company. She expects that it will take at least six months before the framistans are delivered and she receives her payment in francs. She also expects that the franc will fall against the dollar —or depreciate—during that time, eroding the value of her payment when she changes her francs into dollars. (That is, the francs she receives in six months will buy fewer dollars than they would today.)

If she's clever, she will go into the forward exchange market and make a contract to sell francs in six months' time—but at today's price in dollars. That way, if her prediction about the franc falling relative to the dollar is correct, in six months she can offset the money she loses in her framistan deal with her profit in the forward market. (In other words, she has "locked in" the money she expects to make on the framistan sale.)

In this example, the businesswoman has simply hedged herself against a shift in relative currency values. If her anxiety about a depreciating franc is correct, she will have neither lost nor made money. But, like all markets, the forward market can be used for speculating as well as hedging. Speculators having the same anxiety but no business deal to protect might just jump in and make the same contract to sell francs in six months at today's price. And, if the franc depreciates, they will

make money on their contract without an offsetting loss. *See*
FOREIGN EXCHANGE; FUTURES MARKET; HEDGING.

Funding

The act of replacing short-term debt with long-term debt; usually and more specifically, when a company replaces its bank
loans with its own interest-bearing bonds or stocks.

Generally speaking, companies prefer long-term debt (also
called funded debt) because it costs less in interest payments
and is a more stable source of money. Also generally speaking,
investors reward companies which have funded debt by liking
their stocks better than companies which have a lot of un-
funded debt. Thus companies are almost always talking about,
or are in the process of, funding.

Futures Market

A market in which contracts for the future delivery of commodities and financial instruments are bought and sold. Contracts
traded on futures exchanges are called, simply, futures.

A major reason people wish to make a contract in the future
is to lock in a favorable price in the present; that is, to hedge
against an unfavorable price change. Consider a classic example: a wheat farmer has—to use the buzzword—a long position in wheat; he owns it. And he hopes that the price will go
up between the time that he plants it and the time he sells it.

But let's say the price of wheat looks gratifyingly high to him before he starts planting. He can then "lock in" that high price by going into the futures market and arranging to sell his wheat in nine months at the current price.

The reverse is true, of course, for those who don't own the stuff in the present but must buy it in the future. A miller, for instance, who must buy wheat in the future has a—buzzword —short position; she doesn't own it. And she hopes that the price will go down before she makes her purchase. But let's say that she thinks the price of wheat is gratifyingly low nine months before she actually needs it. She will then go into the futures market and buy a contract for wheat for delivery in nine months at that current low price.

In other, fewer words, the chief function of the futures market is to allow buyers and sellers who must wait before they can make their transactions to lay off some of the risk arising from unpredictable price changes. The futures market thus gives buyers and sellers a kind of price insurance. (Like all markets, of course, the futures markets can be used for speculation, too. That's no big deal; it just means that people who have no position to protect in the present make bets about what will happen in the future.)

Futures markets exist for most major commodities and for financial instruments like stock indexes, foreign currencies, and U.S. Treasuries. *See* COMMODITY; FORWARD MARKET; HEDGING; SPOT MARKET.

GINNIE MAE, GOVERNMENT NATIONAL MORTGAGE ASSOCIATION, GNMA

The Government National Mortgage Association, an agency of the Department of Housing and Urban Development, provides financing for low-rent housing. But it is in its money market incarnation that GNMA is known to investors. Here, GNMA guarantees the timely payment of interest and principle on mortgage-backed securities known as Ginnie Maes.

A Ginnie Mae is nothing more than a package made up of individual home mortgages that have been insured by the federal government. The packages are put together, or "pooled," by private mortgage bankers and other financial institutions, and GNMA adds its own guarantee. The resulting new security is then divided into chunks and resold to the public. These securities are called "pass throughs" because the interest and principal payments are made directly to the holders of the chunks every month.

The Ginnie Mae qualifies as a nifty financial innovation because it takes something which is not homogeneous—like a bunch of individual home mortgages—and turns them into one homogeneous instrument which resembles a bond. This process, known as securitization, makes it easier to buy and sell mortgages. And by doing so, it attracts more money into the mortgage market.

Investors like Ginnie Maes because their yields are higher than those of equivalent Treasury bonds despite the fact that they are presumably no riskier than a Treasury bond. They also offer investors a monthly cash flow and good liquidity—it's possible to resell Ginnie Mae chunks to other investors. *See* FANNIE MAE.

Going public

When a closely held company sells shares to the public. Letting outsiders own a piece of the business is not an act of altruism. Firms go public to get money, either because they want to raise additional cash or to allow the original owners to cash out, in the sense that their shares will become more liquid. *See* NEW ISSUE.

Gold standard

A fixed exchange rate brought about when central banks are required to trade a fixed weight of gold for their currencies. In effect, gold becomes a sort of world currency: International debts are settled in gold, and, since currencies are convertible into a fixed amount of gold, differences among them should disappear. But a gold standard does more than function as the world's money—it automatically links changes in a country's money stock with its balance of payments.

Say, for example, that a country, by exporting more than it's importing, is running a surplus in its balance of payments. That surplus means the country is experiencing an inflow of gold. Thus, the central bank can expand the money supply without worrying about having enough gold to cover those paper liabilities.

But consider what happens when the bank prints up a bit more money. An increase in the money supply will push prices up. And higher prices will make it difficult for the country to keep up its strong exports. As the demand for its exports diminishes, so will its balance-of-payments surplus. With less gold to back its currency, the central bank will be forced to cut back on money creation. Thus, prices will fall and equilibrium will be restored. (The reverse is true, of course. A country with a deficit in its balance of payments will be forced to reduce its paper money to correspond to its gold reserves. As prices fall, its exports will become more attractive and it will experience an inflow of gold, thus reducing its balance-of-payments deficit.)

A gold standard, then, controls inflation by disciplining the money creation of central banks; and, by creating stable prices through a fixed exchange rate, it encourages international trade.

If a gold standard can deliver such a tidy package, then why doesn't the world go back to one? Well, perhaps the most powerful reason is that many players feel that a country's balance of payments shouldn't control its money supply. Often a government will wish to run a domestic policy which promotes employment and ignores inflation. Or, to take an extreme example, wars require a lot of money to fight. The United States went off the gold standard during the Civil War, and Great Britain abandoned it during the Napoleonic wars and World War I.

The last serious attempt to hold the major trading nations to a gold standard came in 1944 as part of the Bretton Woods agreement. Here, the dollar was on a gold standard and exchange rates for other currencies were fixed against the dollar. Whether the Bretton Woods system worked or not depends on who you listen to; regardless, it was kiboshed in 1971, when President Nixon put an end to the convertibility of dollars into gold.

The fact that the world flirts with—and often marries—a

gold standard has helped gold retain a certain allure for investors as a kind of safe, always acceptable money. When political trouble threatens in various parts of the world, people buy gold because it is, well, as good as gold.

Too, gold has historically kept its value during times of rising prices. Thus many people watch the price of gold as an indicator of inflation. When the price shoots up—and that verb is intentionally vague, as nobody knows what the correct price of gold should be in terms of, say, the dollar—it is taken as a sign that investors are buying gold as a hedge against inflation. *See* FOREIGN EXCHANGE.

GOODWILL

An intangible quality ascribed to a firm to explain why it's worth more than the market value of its assets minus its liabilities.

If the Framistan Company has $1 million worth of net assets (plant, equipment, cash on hand, and so forth) why would someone be willing to buy it for $1.2 million? Other than bad business judgment—always a possibility—the buyer might think that Framistan has other assets, like a solid reputation or enthusiastic employees, which are worth the extra bucks. These other assets are called goodwill, and their worth is taken to be the difference between the book value of the firm and its purchase price. (Framistan's buyer will carry $200,000 of goodwill as an asset on Framistan's balance sheet.) *See* BALANCE SHEET.

GREENMAIL

See TENDER OFFER.

GROWTH STOCK

Stock in a corporation which is expected to have consistently superior earnings. What distinguishes a growth stock from other "good" stocks is that most of its value comes in the increase in its market price over time as opposed to its cash dividends. *See* CYCLICAL STOCK; DEFENSIVE STOCK; INTEREST RATE SENSITIVE STOCK.

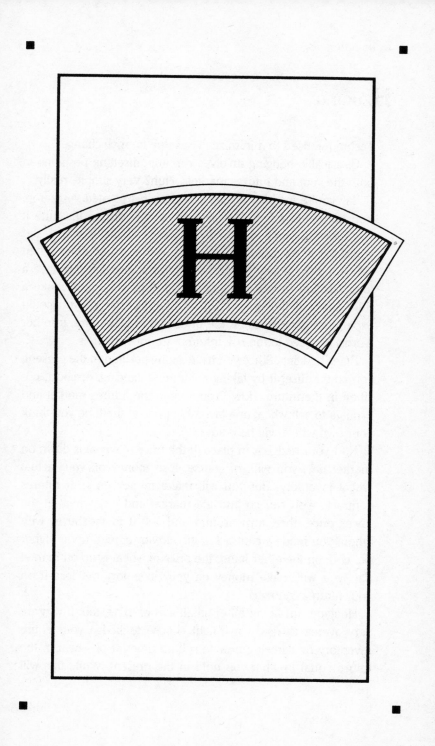

HEDGING

Technique used to minimize losses due to price changes.

Classically, hedging involves running offsetting positions in both the spot and futures markets. Huh? Very simple, really.

Say you're a wheat farmer who has just planted your crop. You know the price of wheat will seesaw during the time it takes for the seeds to grow into harvested, salable wheat. But you don't know whether the price will be up or down when you bring the wheat to market. Put another way, you have a long position in wheat—you own it; thus you could make a huge profit if the price is up at market time, or you could experience a huge loss if the price is down. You are, in other words, exposed to the risk inherent in price changes.

Enter hedging. Since you have a long position in the present, you could offset it by taking a counterbalancing, or short, position in the future. How? You go into the futures market and arrange to sell wheat at a favorable price at the time you think your own wheat will be ready.

Now your hedge is in place. If the price of wheat is down on market day, you will, of course, lose money on your actual wheat inventory. But you will make money on your futures contract—you can go into the market and buy wheat at the lower price, then turn around and sell it to the buyer with whom you made a contract at the already agreed-upon higher price. If, on the other hand, the price of wheat is up on market day, you will make money on your inventory but lose it on your futures contract.

Hedging can be an all-or-small sort of thing, too. If you are very averse to risk, you might choose to hedge your entire inventory by agreeing now to sell an amount of wheat in the future equal to what you hold in the present. While this will protect you against losing money if prices turn against you, it also constrains you from reaping bushels of money if prices skyrocket (because you'll lose an amount of money on your futures equal to what you gained on your inventory). And if you're only a tiny bit averse to risk, you'll simply hedge a smaller portion of your inventory.

Be not deceived by this stripped-down example. In the world of haute finance, hedging can involve exceedingly elaborate, mathematically designed positions and instruments, and it rarely involves the actual delivery of goods, as positions are closed out before contracts expire. But the central purpose still holds: Hedging can reduce risk arising from price fluctuations. *See* FORWARD MARKET; FUTURES MARKET; OPTION; SHORT; SPOT MARKET.

Holding company

A company that exists to own stock in other companies.

A holding company buys a majority position in the stock of other companies in order to control those companies—which then become subsidiaries—as opposed to passively investing in them. Control can mean many things, but basically it means that the holding company supervises the management of its subsidiaries.

HOT MONEY

Term applied to the large, lightning-fast shifts of capital among the world's currencies.

Owners of hot money—often and unfairly described as speculators—sell a country's currency when they expect it to depreciate because the country is on the verge of war, faces an economic slowdown, is experiencing an acceleration in the rate of inflation, or just plain offers inferior investment returns. They buy a country's currency when they expect it to appreciate because the country is politically stable (a safe haven for assets), is about to enjoy a burst of economic growth, or offers superior returns, like high interest rates.

For central bankers and other politicians who are often burned when hot money flows out of their currencies, the term is used disapprovingly. After all, hot money exhibits no national allegiance, and its rushing around can increase the volatility of the foreign exchange markets. Nonetheless, there is absolutely nothing wrong with the owners of money seeking high returns or safe havens.

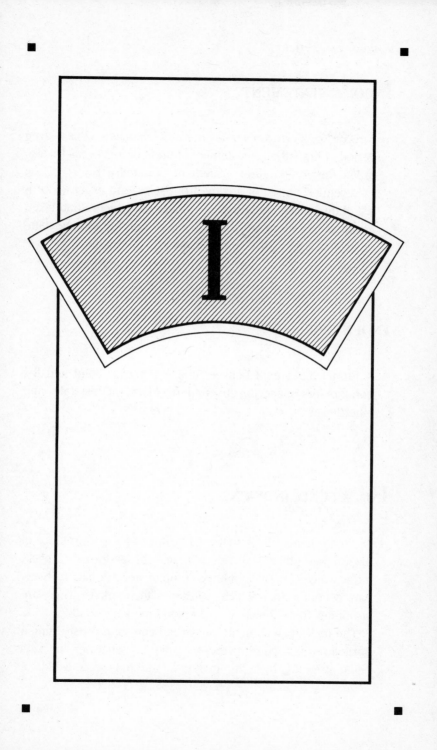

INCOME STATEMENT

A record of a firm's revenues minus its expenses over a given period of time; thus, a statement of profit or loss or, as it's also called, the profit-and-loss statement. (What else?)

Revenues consist of income from sales, and expenses consist of things like operating costs, interest payments, and taxes. Earnings per share are usually recorded on the income statement, too. *See* BALANCE SHEET; FINANCIAL STATEMENTS.

INDENTURE

A formal agreement between the issuer of a bond and the bondholders specifying the maturity date, interest rate, and other terms.

INDEX FUND, INDEXING

An investment vehicle that tries to match the performance of the market—that is, it tries to match the performance of an index which consists of a large group of stocks—like the Standard & Poor's 500—which represents "the market." (There are also index funds which track the bond market.)

The trick in creating an index fund comes in constructing a portfolio which mirrors the securities in whatever index is being used to track the market. Fund managers could, of course, buy every single stock in proportion to its weight in the index, but that can be an operational nightmare. Instead, most managers just concentrate on the stocks that represent the largest weighting in the index.

Indexing is a passive—as opposed to an active—investment strategy. Once the index fund's portfolio is selected, the manager just sits back and watches the fund go up when the market goes up and, of course, go down when the market goes down.

The idea of indexing proceeds from a certain pessimism that active strategies can outperform the market over the long run. Users of index funds figure that since they can't beat the market in the long run, why not just settle for tracking the market —and tracking it on the cheap since the transaction costs of buying and selling securities are less for index funds than they are for active strategies. *See* EFFICIENT MARKET HYPOTHESIS; RANDOM WALK HYPOTHESIS; STANDARD & POOR'S 500 COMPOSITE INDEX.

INDIVIDUAL RETIREMENT ACCOUNT

A sweet device offered by the federal government which encourages people to save for their retirement by giving them tax exemptions.

Congress can, and does, fiddle around with the specific details of IRAs, but the general idea is as follows: A self-employed or employed person earning up to a certain amount can set aside a certain amount of income every year without paying taxes on it. Moreover, the funds in an IRA are allowed to accumulate tax-free until the person retires; then he or she must pay taxes on withdrawals, but presumably he or she will be in a lower tax bracket. (The tax advantage works as long as the person does not withdraw his or her money before age 59½.)

An IRA can be opened at a bank, thrift, mutual fund, or brokerage house; and the money put aside can be held in various forms—stocks, bonds, or money market funds.

No question, a tax shelter that allows both yearly income and/or returns on it to mount up undisturbed for several decades is a good deal. A wise investor can, through the magic of compounding, turn a modest investment into an immodest retirement nest egg. And that, in turn, makes a good deal into a great deal. An IRA is just like having a personal, portable pension plan. It doesn't depend on the vagaries of steady one-employer employment. *See* KEOGH PLAN.

INFLATION

A condition of generally rising prices. Sounds simple enough, but the question of what causes prices to rise has several answers.

One explanation is known as the demand-pull theory because prices are said to be pulled up by a sudden increase in demand, or spending. Monetarists blame demand-pull inflation on monetary policy. Their argument runs like this: When the Federal Reserve pumps out more money than is needed for transactions, the new money will be used to buy assets like stocks and bonds, television sets and cars. Given that the amount of assets has stayed constant, however, this new surge in demand will bid up prices. (More money chasing the same number of goods causes higher prices.)

A second demand-pull theory—one put forward by Keynesians—agrees that the new money will be spent on assets. But they see the primary impact coming from the purchase of bonds: Given that the amount of bonds remains constant, an increase in the demand for bonds will bid up their prices which, of course, will lower interest rates. Lower interest rates, in turn, will encourage more business spending and some consumer spending. Again, the surge in demand for goods will pull prices up.

Another explanation is known as the cost-pull theory because prices are said to be pushed up by a sudden increase in production costs. The wage-push view blames labor unions which negotiate wages higher than can be justified by workers' productivity; companies then have to raise prices of their products to cover these higher labor costs. The profit-push view argues that companies simply raise their prices to increase profits. And the commodity-push view says that an increase in commodity prices—due to political decisions by major producers (like OPEC) or bad weather (like a drought in the grain belt)—will spread through the rest of the economy, pushing up prices in general.

Which theory is correct? Probably all of them. That is, there is no single answer. Inflation can be caused by a number of things, some more important than others at any given moment.

While the causes of inflation may be muddled, its consequences are not. Inflation can be bad for some people and good for others. For example, inflation makes losers out of creditors who are paid back in money that is worth less than when they lent it out. (That is, rising prices means the money buys less.) On the other hand, inflation makes winners out of debtors who can repay their debts in cheaper money.

Some groups are immune from any impact—bad or good. Wages generally keep up with rates of inflation—most union contracts provide for cost-of-living indexing. And Social Security and federal pensions are indexed, as are most private pensions.

There is one kind of inflation, however, that is so disruptive to economic arrangements that it makes for losers across the board—hyperinflation. This is a condition of especially rapid and large increases in prices.

The classic example of hyperinflation occurred in Germany in 1922–1923 when the average rate of inflation was 322% per month. Per month! Cash lost its value so rapidly that people became desperate to exchange it for goods. Workers demanded their wages twice a day in order to shop at midday because, by the end of the day, prices would be higher. And— or so the joke goes—beer drinkers ordered two mugs at a time because the second beer would go flat slower than its price would rise.

INSIDE INFORMATION

Nonpublic knowledge of something which will materially affect the financial status of a firm and the price of its stock.

There's nothing wrong with inside information, per se. At any one time, there are lots of people who are privy to inside information—corporate officers, lawyers, investment bankers, secretaries, taxi drivers. What's wrong—and illegal—is for people to profit by trading stock on information that has not been fully disclosed. *See* INSIDER TRADING.

INSIDER TRADING

The strictly illegal practice of buying and/or selling stock on the basis of nonpublic information. Strictly illegal it may be, but strictly defined it is not. And I'm not just being cute, either. Consider:

An insider can be anybody whose employment at a company makes him privy to nonpublic information which will, once it is made public, have an impact on the price of the company's stock. That encompasses everybody from corporate officers to secretaries. Increasingly, however, the word insider also refers to "temporary" insiders—anyone whose employment at a firm engaged in doing business with the company makes him or her privy to material, nonpublic information. That encompasses employees of the company's investment banking firm, law firm, accounting firm, and so on.

Trading on inside information refers to the practice in which the above-mentioned insiders either buy shares of the company if they expect the information to boost the price, or sell shares if they expect the news to depress the price.

Okay. Assume, then, that the definition of insider is clear despite all the varieties of people who can be considered insiders; and assume that any trading related to inside information by them is illegal. What if one of these insiders tells his sister-in-law and she trades? Has she become an insider? Has the actual insider violated the trading prohibition even though he does not directly profit from his sister-in-law's trade? Hmmmm. (And I haven't even touched on the hot debate over what, exactly, constitutes "material, nonpublic" information.)

At any rate, the only sure way to know whether or not you may be in violation of the law is if the Securities and Exchange

Commission says so. And if you are found guilty by the courts, you could pay a fine or you could pay a fine *and* go to jail.

Insider trading on information which has been fully disclosed is legal. But insiders—corporate officers and large stockholders—are required to tell the SEC when they trade the stock. What could be more legal? *See* INSIDE INFORMATION; SECURITIES AND EXCHANGE COMMISSION.

INSTITUTIONAL INVESTOR

An organization—as opposed to an individual—which has a huge pool of money to invest.

Institutional investors come in many guises: corporate and public pension plans, insurance companies, mutual funds, bank trust departments, endowments. Whatever the guise, the mechanism is the same: Individuals voluntarily (mutual funds) or involuntarily (pension plans) give their money to an institution, which then invests it.

The form itself is interesting because people are increasingly relying on these institutions to invest their money and/or provide for their retirement. As a general rule, however, the more money an institutional investor has, the more conservative—and less successful in out-performing the market—its investment strategy is.

INSURANCE

A clever way of spreading risk so that an individual doesn't have to bear the entire financial burden of a catastrophe, whether the catastrophe is minor (a broken finger) or major (a wrecked house).

At its simplest, the mechanism whereby financial risk is spread from one individual to a group works like this: Each member of the group pays a tiny portion of what the catastrophe would cost into a common pool; then, when disaster strikes the unlucky member of the group, he or she can claim the money in the pool.

So much for theory. In practice, insurance takes the form of a contract between an individual and an insurance company. The contract, called a policy, specifies the amount the company must pay out in case of disaster (the coverage) and the amount the insured person must pay in to be covered (the premium). The nature of the disaster which will trigger the payout is also specified, usually in mind-numbing detail.

The size of the premium is determined by the insurance company's assessment of how likely it is that the disaster will occur. The more likely the disaster, the higher the premium. Thus, in the case of auto accident insurance, a teenage boy will pay more for his coverage than an adult woman.

Insurance companies usually specialize in different types of insurance: Some provide life insurance, others offer protection against fires and earthquakes.

INTEREST

The price paid by borrowers for using lenders' money over time. Or, more briefly, the cost of borrowing money.

Interest is expressed as a rate, or percentage. If I lend you $100 (the principal) for one year and you pay me $10 (the interest payment), the interest is 10 percent. Unless I am a loan shark, however, I cannot set the interest rate above the market, or prevailing, rate. Of course, that begs the question of what determines the market rate and what determines whether the market rate is high or low.

In general, the level of interest rates depends on the supply of loanable funds and the demand for those funds. If, for example, everybody is spending like mad and saving very little —and borrowing to finance their spending—then interest rates will be high. That's another way of saying that when credit is scarce, its price will be bid up.

The level of interest rates also depends on something called the inflation premium, that is, the risk that inflation will erode the value of the money before it is paid back. In times of high rates of inflation, for instance, loans that are made for relatively long periods of time will have higher interest rates to compensate lenders for the damage done by inflation.

Beyond supply-and-demand conditions in the credit market, there are a number of other things which determine specific interest rates, such as the rates on credit cards, government loans, business loans, and loans made to consumers by banks. Most important, interest rates depend on how liquid the loan instrument is and how likely the borrower is to default on it.

Consider, for example, federal government debt. A five-year bond is very liquid—you can get somebody else to buy it without too much trouble—and the chance of default is almost zero. Then consider a consumer loan; it is quite illiquid, and the chances of default are relatively high. Obviously, then, the interest rate—or the price of the money—on the consumer loan should be higher than on the government bond because the lender's return on his money must compensate him for the illiquidity and the risk of default.

One further note: Interest payments can be figured several ways. Simple interest is when the payments are calculated only on the original principal amount. Compound interest is when the previously accrued interest payments are included in the principal amount. And continuous compounding is when the interest payments are added to the principal amount so frequently as to be continuous, as opposed to being added at discrete intervals like quarterly or yearly. *See* PRIME RATE.

INTEREST RATE SENSITIVE STOCK

Exactly as it sounds: common stock in an industry which is responsive to changes in interest rates. The fortunes of financial companies like banks and savings and loans, for example, are closely tied to interest rates. When rates go up, their earnings usually go down and so does the price of their stocks— and vice versa. *See* CYCLICAL STOCK; DEFENSIVE STOCK; GROWTH STOCK.

Intrinsic Value

The "true" worth of an asset as opposed to its market price.

This is one of those buzzwords which should excite suspicion in the hearer. Especially since it's most often heard coming from the mouth of a broker who wants to convince you to buy an "undervalued" stock. Sure, it's possible that the market, in its collective wisdom, has misunderstood the true worth of the Flims-o Company; but beware that this possibility may not be translatable into cash when you want to sell your shares.

Investment

Strictly and properly defined, investment refers to any expenditure to which benefits will accrue in the future.

Economic investment means something more specific than financial investment; it usually includes the construction of new office buildings, factories, houses, and apartment buildings, new equipment, and increases in inventories. The term "net investment" means gross investment after allowances for depreciation. Economic investment, then, applies to expenditures on capital goods.

Financial investment includes expenditures for stocks or bonds or, for that matter, any outlay of money which is expected to result in some financial gain. If expectations are thwarted and money is lost, then the investment is said to have been a bad one. *See* BATH; SPECULATION.

INVESTMENT BANK

A sort of middleperson between the corporation that issues securities and the public that buys them. (While that definition should suffice, be warned that investment bankers are rather smug and taken with what they would define as their role as financial intermediaries in raising long-term capital and thus providing for the future of the nation . . . and so on and so forth.)

Investment banks are, well, for investment. They are different from commercial banks, which also do some forms of investment but do a lot of other things, too. The general function of an investment bank is to advise its clients, usually corporations, on how to raise long-term capital, usually by selling stock, and then to assist them, usually by selling and distributing that stock. Often a bank will buy the stock outright and then sell it to individuals and institutions. In this case, the bank is underwriting the securities; that is, assuming the risk that it may not be able to unload the stock at a higher price than it paid.

INVESTMENT COMPANY (*or* TRUST)

General name given to any organization which sells shares to the public and then invests the money in other companies. *See* CLOSED-END MUTUAL FUND; OPEN-END MUTUAL FUND.

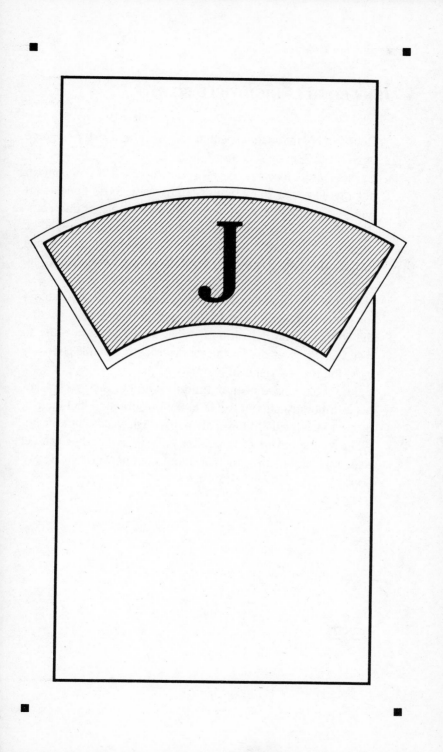

Junk Bond (*or* HIGH-YIELD BOND)

Debt of a company that is either rated below investment grade or is unrated; in other words, junk.

There are two ways to get a junk bond. If a company in dubious financial shape issues bonds, then those bonds start out life as junk. Or, if the finances of a formerly sound company turn bad, then their outstanding bonds are downgraded; these are sometimes called fallen angels. (Issuing junk bonds has also become a favorite ploy in financing hostile corporate takeovers.)

Buying the junk bonds of what are, after all, considered junky companies, is risky since there is a high probability that the company will default on its obligations. Thus, in order to compensate investors for this credit risk, junk bonds generally carry the highest yields in the market.

Junk bonds have been around forever, but their recent status as a hot investment is due to the presumption that the risk of default is actually lower than the high yields indicate. In other words, buyers of junk bonds presume that they can get high returns on investment without commensurate risk. *See* BOND.

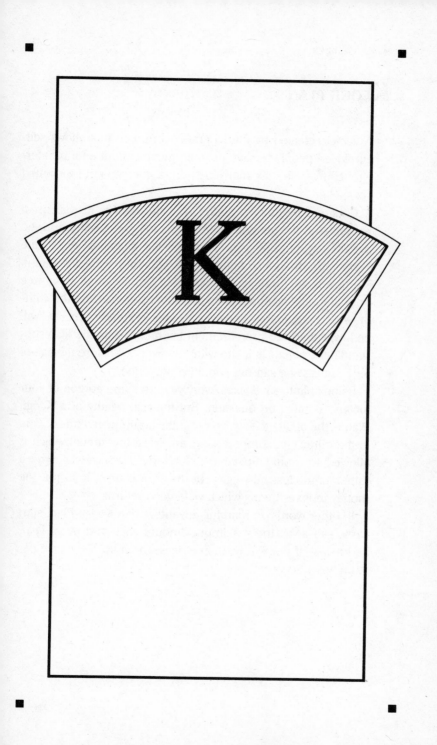

KEOGH PLAN

A vehicle created by the federal government that allows self-employed people to save for retirement without a lot of interference from the tax man. In short, a government-sanctioned tax shelter.

Congress frequently diddles with the specific provisions of Keoghs, but the general outline is as follows: a self-employed person can set aside a certain percentage of his or her income every year, up to a certain amount, without paying taxes on it. Moreover, the funds in a Keogh Plan can accumulate tax-free until the person retires; then she must pay taxes on the withdrawals. Presumably, however, her postretirement tax rate will be lower than her preretirement tax rate. (There are also substantial tax penalties if she withdraws money before the age of 59½, unless she satisfies certain conditions.)

Being able to save taxes every year on some portion of your income is nifty, no question. But the real beauty of a Keogh Plan is the ability to save taxes on the accumulated funds. Due to the miracle of compounding, a modest investment which is allowed to mount up tax-free for forty years can become a rather immodest nest egg. The trick, of course, is to put the money in investments which yield good returns.

In other words, to reap full advantage of a Keogh Plan, start early, salt away the maximum amount each and every year, and invest, if not wisely, then at least carefully. *See* INDIVIDUAL RETIREMENT ACCOUNT.

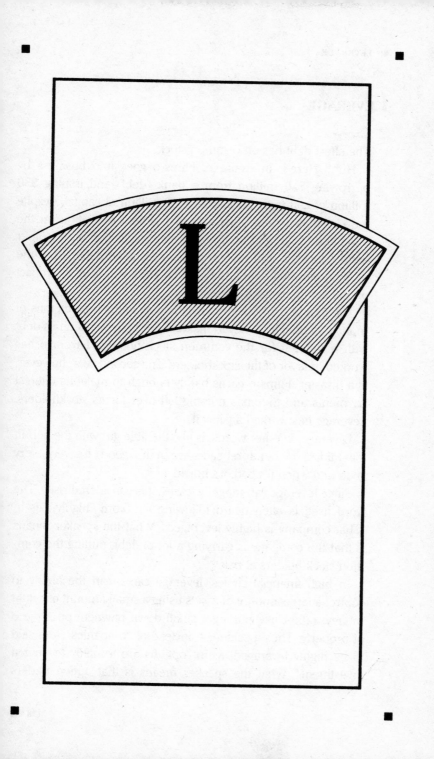

LEVERAGE

The effect debt has on common stock.

Huh? Here's an example. Flims-o goes into business by borrowing $50 million from a bank (debt) and issuing $50 million of common stock. This $100 million of capital, despite the fact that it represents a fixed payment obligation on the one hand (debt) and no fixed payment obligation on the other hand (stock), is 100 million indistinguishable dollars; but the division between debt and common stock will have an impact on the common stock from now on.

The first year of business is fabulous. Flims-o earns tons of money—enough money to make interest payments on its debt with plenty left for the common stock holders. Leverage has worked in favor of the stockholders. The second year, however, is a disaster. Flims-o earns barely enough to make its interest payments and thus has nothing left over for its stockholders. Leverage has worked against it.

Leverage, in other words, is like the little girl with the curl in the middle of her forehead—when it's good, it's very, very good and when it's bad, it's horrid.

Since leverage can magnify losses, it is considered risky. The word itself is often heard following the word "highly," as in "That company is highly leveraged." What the speaker means is that the company is carrying a lot of debt, putting the common stock holders at risk.

In high financial circles, leverage can mean the ability to control a large amount of assets using a small amount of actual money, rather like putting a small down payment on a piece of property. Thus, positions—instead of companies—are said to be highly leveraged, as in "options are a highly leveraged investment." What the speaker means is that option traders control assets which have value much greater than the amount of money they have invested. *See* MARGIN.

LEVERAGED BUYOUT *or* LBO

Term of art describing the practice of turning a publicly held company into a privately held one by buying out its stockholders where the buyout involves a lot of debt financing, using the company's assets as collateral for that debt.

A typical LBO works like this: A group of the company's current managers decides that it would be better off in private hands. (Translation: The price of the company's stock seems cheap and they'd like to get their hands on it.) The buyers then raise the money to buy the company by issuing debt. (Translation: The buyers don't want to spend their own money, so they issue a bunch of junk bonds which, of course, gives them lots of leverage.) The buyers show their faith in the worth of the company by pledging its own assets to back up its debt. (Translation: They have leveraged the company to the hilt without risking very much themselves.)

As investments go, this is a nifty one. If all goes well, the new owners can resell the company to the public for many times what they "paid" for it. If all goes poorly, the new owners escape without much financial damage. Any losers if all goes bad? Sure. The company—to the extent that it is a productive entity—and the holders of the bonds—to the extent that the sale of the company's assets doesn't fully cover their investment.

LIABILITY

A debt obligation, or amount of money owed.

The formal designation "liability" found on business balance sheets typically takes two forms: short-term and long-term (or, often, deferred). A short-term liability is one which must be paid off within a year—like taxes or interest payments; a long-term one is one that can be carried on the books for longer than a year—like deferred taxes or a mortgage. Liabilities appear on the right-hand side of the balance sheet, assets on the left. In fact, the reason balance sheets are called balance sheets is because liabilities, plus retained earnings, will always equal assets. *See* ASSET; BALANCE SHEET.

LIMITED LIABILITY, LIMITED PARTNER

The first "limited" applies to the stockholders of a corporation who are not liable for the debts of the corporation, and the second "limited" to the partners in a partnership who are not liable for the debts of a partnership. In the case of bankruptcy, for example, both shareholders and partners will lose whatever they invested, but they won't have to reach into their pockets to pay off creditors.

LIMIT ORDER

Type of order given by a customer to a broker to buy or sell something at a specific price.

If, for example, the customer wants to buy stock, then the limit order would be to buy at no more than the customer's set price, although buying for less than that price would be quite okay. And if the customer wants to sell stock, then the order would be to sell at no less than the customer's set price, although selling for more than that price would also be quite okay. The idea here is that the customer thinks the stock is either worth less or more than its current market price and is confident that the market price will eventually move more into line with his or her thinking. *See* MARKET ORDER; STOP ORDER.

LINE OF CREDIT

The result of an agreement between a bank and a borrower, usually a business, that allows the withdrawal of a specific maximum amount of money over a specific amount of time. Lines of credit, which are really loans, are extended subject to certain conditions, for example that borrowers have to keep a specific amount of money in their checking accounts.

LIQUIDITY

The ease or speed with which an asset can be turned into cash money.

Liquidity depends on the nature of the market for any particular asset. Some assets, like shares in IBM or General Motors, are very liquid—owners can sell them for cash in a few minutes. Other assets, like homes or airplanes, are illiquid—owners must wait awhile before buyers are found. The only asset which is completely liquid is, of course, cash; even a check drawn on a bank in Algiers might be completely illiquid when the holder appears at a bank window in Des Moines.

A business is said to be liquid when it has enough cash to pay back its creditors. An illiquid business runs the risk of not being able to pay its expenses on a timely basis and, in fact, of going bankrupt. Hence, when a business goes bankrupt, and its assets are sold, the process is known as liquidation.

Liquidity is also one of those measures that investors use to evaluate an investment in something. Not only do they want to know how liquid their investment is once they have made it, but they use the liquidity of the enterprise to determine the risk that their investment will go sour. One of the heavy-duty measures is called the liquidity—no surprise—ratio. This ratio casts the liquid assets of the business over the current liabilities. If the ratio is too small—a subjective judgment—then potential investors may decide that investment in the company is too risky. If it appears large, then investors figure the company can at least pay its bills in the short term.

LISTED SECURITY

A stock or bond which is registered with a stock exchange and therefore can be traded on that exchange.

Corporations want to have their securities listed on an exchange for various reasons, but mostly it's because listed stocks are easier for investors to trade than unlisted ones. Listing thus makes it easier for corporations to attract a broader following and raise new capital. Corporations also think that this greater visibility bestows prestige.

For their part, exchanges require that companies meet certain standards for listed securities, which mostly have to do with the size of the corporation and its issued stock.

Most exchanges have an actual floor on which security trading is done. There are, however, totally electronic trading markets which do not require buy and sell orders to cross in one particular location. In fact, there is a hot debate about which type of trading system provides the best execution for buyers and sellers. *See* STOCK EXCHANGE; UNLISTED SECURITY.

LONG

Expression indicating the ownership of stock.

This is one of those buzzwords which can only be truly understood—and appreciated—in context. When you buy a stock, you have a "long" position in that stock: as in "I am long that stock." Long is also a term indicating that you are bullish about the prospects of the purchased stock. When you buy a stock, you do so because you are optimistic that its price will go up: as in "Boy oh boy, am I long that stock." Being long is the opposite of being short. *See* SHORT.

LOOSE MONEY

One of those colorful phrases which perfectly captures a complicated idea. "Loose" refers to the monetary policy undertaken by the Federal Reserve and "money" refers to the amount of money in the economy.

When the Fed decides to make credit readily available to borrowers, it increases the supply of money. This is supposed to lower interest rates, which in turn makes borrowing attractive. In other words, loose money means that the Fed has relaxed its grip on the growth of money.

The opposite of loose money is tight money. *See* EASY MONEY; THE FED; TIGHT MONEY.

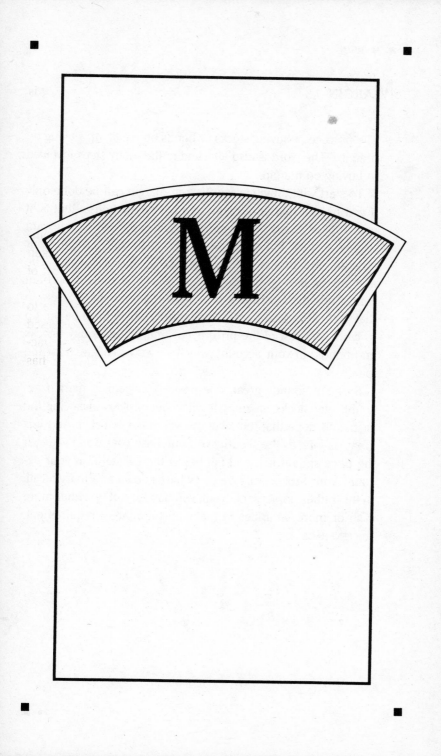

MARGIN

The practice of buying stocks or bonds on credit, or "buying on margin." The word is also attached to the many steps involved in buying on margin.

To start with, buying securities on margin can be done only if you have a margin account at a brokerage house; that is, if your broker grants you overdraft privileges. Then, if you want to buy a stock but need more cash than you have in your account, the broker will automatically lend it to you. The amount of money which can be lent in a margin account comes under the heading of margin requirement; it refers to that part of the total price of the security which must be put up in cash. The rest of the price is covered by the equity (stocks and bonds) in your account, which serves as collateral for the loan.

So far it sounds great, doesn't it? You open a margin account, buy stocks on margin with your broker advancing the cash, and hope that the leverage will make you rich. And it *is* great, as long as the security you purchase goes up in value. If the price should fall, and fall below the collateral in your account, your broker will give you what's known as a margin call. In this rather unpleasant event, you have to put up either more cash or more securities to maintain the margin requirement. *See* LEVERAGE.

MARKET

Formally, what is created when buyers and sellers get together to trade; informally, shorthand for the stock market, as defined by the Dow Jones Industrial Averages.

In other words, "market" is one of those all-purpose terms which can refer to lots of things. But since this book deals with money and finance, it seems reasonable to discuss the financial markets. Here, buyers are lenders or savers, and sellers are borrowers or debtors, and the financial markets bring them together through a variety of instruments.

The term "financial markets" itself encompasses a bunch of specific markets, depending on what instruments are traded. There are, for instance, the capital market and the money market, the bond market and the stock market, the spot market and the futures market, the options market and the foreign exchange market.

There are a number of more or less rigorous economic definitions on what makes a good market; generally, however, a good market attracts many players, offers many instruments, and has frequent trading and low transactions costs (the costs of matching buyers and sellers). The existence of "good" markets is more than just an academic exercise, however; the better the market, the better the allocation of scarce resources (in this case, investment money) to their best use. *See* CAPITAL MARKET; EFFICIENT MARKET HYPOTHESIS; FINANCIAL INTERMEDIARY; MONEY MARKET.

MARKET ORDER

An order given to a broker to buy or sell something at whatever the price is when the order reaches the market. (As in "Hey! Buy me a hundred shares of IBM at market!") *See* LIMIT ORDER; STOP ORDER.

MERGER

The combination of two or more companies through the direct acquisition of the mergee's assets by the merge-or; the merge-or also assumes the mergee's liabilities.

There are as many ways to effect a combination as there are —if you'll excuse me—to skin a cat. But basically it's either done by the merge-or paying cash for the mergee's securities or by an exchange of securities.

That's how it is done. Why is it done? Well, mergers are considered a quick-and-dirty way for the merge-or company to grow bigger; a process which is formally called "growing through external means."

The word "merger" is often combined with the word "acquisition," as in "mergersandacquisitions" or M&As. Many financial institutions have departments which are devoted to M&A activity—less politely called takeovers. *See* ACQUISITION.

MONETARISM

School of thought which holds that changes in the supply of money are the chief determinant of economic activity.

The monetarist view of the way the world works can be simply put. Too much money in the economy leads to increases in the general price level (inflation) and to booms, while too little leads to decreases in prices and to busts; and up-and-down changes in the money supply lead to an up-and-down economy. The effect of the money supply is not immediate, however; there's a long and uncertain period of time before it has an impact on the economy.

No surprise, then, that monetarists are utterly fixated on the Federal Reserve: The Fed, as the author of monetary policy, must—perforce—be the most important player in determining the course of economy.

But their fixation takes the form of severe vexation. Because, according to monetarist theory, the Fed can never be sure when its policies will be effective, they don't believe it has any business trying to manage the economy through changes in the money supply. Especially since they believe that the Fed's activist policy causes many of the fluctuations.

Thus, monetarism argues that the Fed should simply aim at supplying the economy with money at a constant rate of growth. Indeed, if the Fed turned into a little robot, printing new money at around 3 percent a year, monetarists would be well satisfied.

During the late 1960s and 1970s, monetarists warned that the excess money creation would result in inflation. They were ignored. They were dismissed as naive. They were, however, right. During the early eighties, monetarists warned that excess money creation would again result in inflation. This time many people listened to them. They were, however, wrong. And nowadays most people have taken to ignoring them again. *See* THE FED.

MONEY

Any generally accepted means of payment in exchange for goods and services.

Money replaced barter which, as a system of payments, was extremely awkward. With money, people can directly exchange their labor for money and then exchange their money for steaks or haircuts. That makes money incredibly more efficient than barter, in which people might have to exchange their labor for bananas and then find other people who like bananas enough to be willing to exchange their steaks for them.

Of course—and this is the point—even bananas could be money if everybody accepted them as a medium of exchange. Then anybody with steaks would be happy to exchange steaks for bananas, knowing that they, in turn, could easily exchange those bananas for haircuts. Individual taste for bananas would not be an issue.

At any rate, money can be anything people are willing to accept—pieces of paper, wampum, or bananas—as a medium of exchange. But money has two other roles: as a unit of account and as a store of value.

A unit of account means that the units in which money is measured—dollars and cents for paper money, ounces and pounds for banana money—become the price at which all goods and services can be valued. Thus, a steak can be said to be worth $10 or twenty pounds of bananas, a haircut worth

$20 or forty pounds of bananas. Furthermore, having a unit into which everything can be translated makes it possible to combine various goods and services. For example, the prices of all the goods and services in the economy can be added together to produce one measure of economic activity, or GNP. (Nothing more than the old trick of combining apples and oranges.)

A store of value means that money can be used to warehouse wealth for future purchases. Sellers will accept money today, even if they have no immediate plans to spend it, because they assume it will keep its value over time. In this case, of course, bananas would make lousy money—they might simply rot away before they could be spent. Not that paper money is perfect. Inflation can erode the value of paper money just as surely as oxidation erodes the value of bananas. Just not as quickly. (Usually.) *See* BARTER.

MONEY MARKET

The financial market for short-term borrowing and investment. Just like other markets, the money market serves to link up buyers and sellers. In this case, the buyers are lenders like banks, corporations, governments, pension plans, and insurance companies, and the sellers are borrowers, who, not surprisingly, are often the same cast of characters as the buyers.

The securities, or instruments, which link up these borrowers and lenders range from the familiar and more or less standard stuff like bank certificates of deposit, short-term government notes, and federal agency securities to the more arcane and unique like repurchase agreements (repos), bankers' acceptances, and Eurodollar deposits. And, just as the instruments vary, so does what is meant by short-term—anywhere from overnight to, strictly speaking, under one year.

Because these instruments are so highly liquid, they are considered less risky than the longer-term paper that makes up the capital market. But that only means that they are less subject to interest rate risk (the danger that interest rates will change radically), not less subject to default risk (the danger that the borrower can't make good on the debt).

The money market is an efficient mechanism for three types of players. It serves big banks, which try to utilize all their available cash and thus often have an intense need to borrow short-term sums. It serves small banks which are run more conservatively and thus often have idle cash. It permits the U.S. Treasury to be more flexible in its borrowing. And it also aids corporations which experience variable demands on their internal cash flow, thus leaving them sometimes in need of short-term money and other times flush with it.

The money market is a wholesale market where dealers and brokers do business for their clients by screaming to other dealers and brokers on telephones. Small investors have access to the money market through money market mutual funds, which can invest in many of these money market securities. *See* CAPITAL MARKET.

MONEY SUPPLY

The amount of cash money and noncash money in the economy at any one time.

There are four categories, or definitions, of money. M1 covers the most liquid form—currency held outside banks and checking accounts held inside banks and other financial institutions. M2 adds in small savings accounts, money market mutual funds, overnight bank repurchase agreements, and Eurodollars. M3 adds in large savings deposits and long-term repurchase agreements. And the last category, L, adds in instruments like U.S. Treasury bills, savings bonds, and commercial paper. These four categories are familiarly known as the monetary aggregates.

Measuring the amount of money in the economy—and controlling it—is an often thankless task which falls to the Federal Reserve. Essentially, the Fed decides at what rate the economy ought to be supplied with money and then sets what are called targets for each of the Ms. (Say the GNP is growing at 3 percent a year, then the Fed might decide to let the money supply grow apace.) Not all categories are equal, however. M1 rates lots of attention, M3 hardly any. To find out why the Fed should do this, and what difference it makes in the grand scheme of things, *see* THE FED; LOOSE MONEY; MONETARISM; TIGHT MONEY.

MORTGAGE

A legal agreement under which a specific property becomes the security for a loan. The creditor becomes, in a sense, the owner of the property until the loan is paid back, although the debtor (usually) possesses the property. If the loan isn't paid back, of course, the creditor can take possession.

A mortgage—or more properly, a mortgage loan—is the traditional way to finance the purchase of a home. The institution granting the mortgage is actually giving a loan, and while the mortgagor can live in the house during the life of the loan, the holder of the mortgage can evict the mortgagor if he or she fails to make payments on the loan.

Usually the mortgagor pays a lump sum—called the down payment—up front and then makes timely payments of the principal and interest until the loan is repaid, or amortized. Usually. The market for mortgage loans has become very inventive and almost all aspects of the transaction can be tailor-made. Interest payments, principal payments, and down payments can all vary; for example, with adjustable rate mortgages, the interest rate component of the monthly payment goes up or down with the rate of inflation.

MULTINATIONAL CORPORATION

A firm which produces and markets products in many nations.

MUNICIPAL BOND, MUNI, *or* TAX-EXEMPT

Debt issued by any tax-exempt entity like a state, county, city, or school district on which interest payments (but not any capital gain) are tax-exempt.

States and localities, just like individuals and businesses, often experience an intense desire for money they don't have. So states and localities, just like individuals and businesses, go out to borrow the necessary funds. And states and localities, just like individuals and businesses, sometimes find that they cannot pay back these debts. Thus, even though munis carry nifty tax savings, an investment in them should be viewed through the same narrowed eye as any other investment; to wit, the returns offered should be high enough to compensate for the risk of losing the original stake.

There are two types of munis: general obligation bonds backed by something magisterially known as the full faith and credit—read the taxing power—of the issuing entity, and revenue bonds backed by the revenues of a specific project, agency, or tax. Most observers think that the former is less subject to the risk of default than the latter. But even then, the most intrepid investors would find the task of evaluating the full faith and credit of issuing agencies daunting. Luckily, they don't have to.

Investors can rely on bond credit ratings by Standard & Poor's or Moody's. Bonds thought to have the best credit risk are given a triple-A designation—or the wonderfully appropriate Aaa, which looks like an ahhhh of relief. Bonds which seem speculative are rated double-B—or the also wonderfully appropriate Ba, which looks like bah. And those with the worst rating are given a single C.

Too, cautious investors might buy bonds which have been insured by a private company, like the American Municipal Bond Assurance Corporation or the Municipal Bond Insurance Association.

Beyond the wealth of entities which can, and do, issue tax-exempts, the bonds themselves come in a wealth of flavors. Terms vary from under a year to over thirty years, although some munis have call provisions, which means that the issuer can redeem them before their stated payback date. Dollar amounts range from $1,000 to $1,000,000.

One last note on muni jargon: The words "City of New York, 5 of 99 at 5.25 percent" mean that bonds issued by New York

City, carrying an interest rate of 5 percent and maturing in 1999, are priced to yield 5.25 percent; since the yield is higher than the rate of interest specified on the bond, the bond is priced at a discount to par, or lower than its face value. *See* BOND; BOND YIELD.

MUTUAL FUND

See CLOSED-END MUTUAL FUND; OPEN-END MUTUAL FUND.

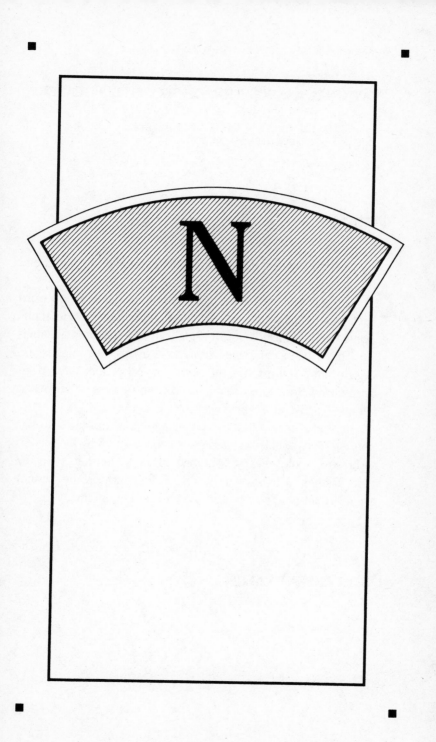

NATIONAL ASSOCIATION OF SECURITIES DEALERS

See OVER-THE-COUNTER MARKET.

NET-NET

A marvelously useful phrase meaning that after all is said and done, this is what it comes to.

Net-net itself has perfectly respectable origins in the word net. Net means whatever is left after all relevant considerations have been deducted. Net worth is what is left after total liabilities have been subtracted from total assets; net sales is the figure after returns, freight costs, and discounts have been subtracted from gross sales. In fact, the process of deducting items to arrive at the net is called netting out.

Net-net is most often used after a long, complicated and/or boring recital of facts or figures. It is used either by the reciter, who says apologetically, "Anyway, this is the net-net . . ." or by the listener, who says impatiently, "Well, what's the net-net here?" (Net-net has replaced the phrase "bottom line.")

NET PRESENT VALUE

See DISCOUNTING.

NET WORTH

The value of a company after total liabilities are subtracted from total assets.

If that number is positive, then the company is said to have a positive net worth. If the number is negative, then the company is said to have a negative net worth, a condition which usually leads to bankruptcy.

Net worth is a measure of how much equity the owners have in the business, how much they have invested, and how much profit has stayed in. Thus, purists refer to it as owners' equity, which is also the term used on financial statements.

NEW ISSUE, NEW ISSUE MARKET

The stock of companies when they go public and that part of the capital market in which this stock is traded.

Private companies with good growth prospects often find that if they are going to realize their potential they need more capital than they can generate internally or borrow. Thus these companies will go public by offering shares to general investors. The public gets a piece of the action, and the company gets a chunk of cash.

The new issue market is the place where legendary investment bets are made. This is where your brother-in-law bought 10,000 $2 shares of the company that, in only five years, is turning out to be the new Xerox. (And if your brother-in-law is like most successful new issue investors, he bought a boat that he christened with the stock's name.)

But along with the possibilities of giant returns, investment bets here carry a giant risk: not only the risk that the hapless company might go bankrupt, but that the company itself is, politely put, a scam. Although even the most savvy investor is likely to get burned in the new issue market, novices should probably stay away from companies that haven't actually started making products, have no growth record, carry a lot of debt, or are counting on a change in government policy to make them profitable. *See* GOING PUBLIC.

NEW YORK STOCK EXCHANGE

Marketplace located in New York City (on Wall Street, as it happens) where people gather to trade stocks.

The clearest way to explain how stocks are traded on the NYSE is with an example. If you want to buy some IBM (a company which is listed on the NYSE), you call your broker and say "Buy a hundred shares of IBM at the market price." Your broker will call her representative at the NYSE, who will then rush over to the exchange specialist whose job it is to maintain a market in IBM stock. The representative will buy a hundred shares from the specialist, who matches your order up with a seller who is also working through a brokerage house and its representative.

The New York Stock Exchange is the biggest, most prestigious of the U.S. stock exchanges. And because it has traditionally maintained high standards for its listed companies, lots of companies and investors have come to look on Big Board listing as an index of financial importance and approval.

Nonetheless, any market is only as good as its trading system. And good trading systems should provide investors with liquidity, low transaction costs, and prices which reflect the broadest consensus possible. And here the Big Board has its doubters.

The exchange trading system is theoretically an auction market. That means all buying and selling is supposed to take place in one spot—on the floor of the exchange where the specialist stands at his post. All interested buyers and sellers are supposed to meet there and arrive at prices through the auction process. (If no buyer wants to buy IBM at the seller's offering price, then the seller will keep lowering his price until he finds a buyer.)

That's the theory. But not quite the practice.

For starters, trades involving big chunks of stocks—called block trades—are handled not on the floor of the exchange but through brokerage houses or investment banks, which offer the blocks to buyers in a negotiated arrangement. Further, there are times on the floor of the exchange where no auction is possible. For example, when bad news on a stock means there are no buyers, only sellers, the specialist is supposed to stand ready to buy for his own inventory. Supposed to. On those occasions when the specialist doesn't have enough money—or a strong enough stomach—to buy, then trading is halted and there is, in effect, no market at all.

Events like these have eroded the power of the NYSE and prompted critics to suggest that the marketplace of the future belongs to highly automated trading systems like the NASDAQ in the over-the-counter market.

The debate over which trading system delivers the best market for its users has been a long and—often—an acrimonious one. But unless it is settled against the NYSE, the Big Board and its specialist system will continue to dominate popular imagination as a quintessential Wall Street institution. *See* LISTED SECURITY; OVER-THE-COUNTER MARKET; STOCK EXCHANGE.

Nominal

The value of something, unadjusted for factors which may reduce or increase its real value.

Two uses here: The nominal value of a security is the price which appears on its face, which may, of course, be different than its market price; and the nominal rate of interest, which is the rate unadjusted for the impact of inflation.

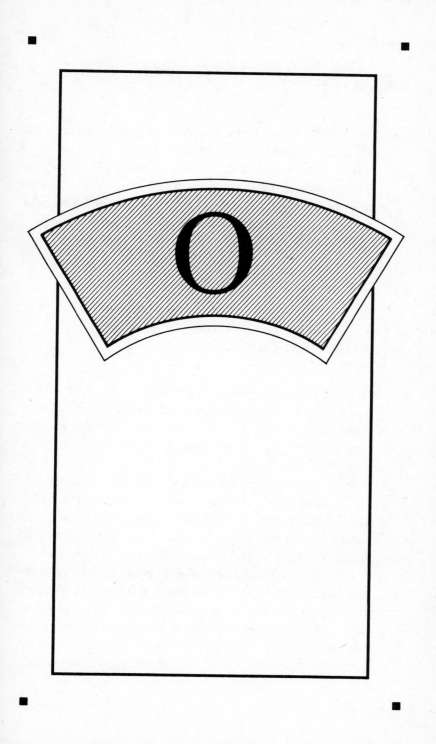

ODD LOT

An amount of stock that is less than the trading unit required by a stock exchange, usually 100 shares.

Odd is in the eye of the beholder. If you want to buy an even number of shares—called a round lot—of 200, you may pay an odd amount of money. If you want to invest an even amount of money—as in a round number like $2,000—you may end up buying an odd lot of stock. *See* BLOCK TRADE.

OPEN-END MUTUAL FUND *or* OPEN-END INVESTMENT COMPANY

An investment organization which invests money from the public in securities; in return for the money, the mutual fund issues units, or shares, of the investment portfolio which it stands ready to repurchase for the net asset value of the portfolio.

As its name implies, the number of shares in an open-end fund is open-ended, unlike a closed-end mutual fund, where the number of shares is fixed. These shares cannot be traded on any market and are always worth total assets minus total liabilities divided by the number of shares.

Typically, open-end funds offer investors a family of funds —the cozy name given to a group of funds with different investment objectives. Some funds will invest only in common stock, some only in bonds, some in a little of everything. Typically, investors can transfer their money from fund to fund within the family with little hassle or expense (although mutual funds charge investors a tariff known as a management fee). *See* CLOSED-END MUTUAL FUND.

OPEN-MARKET OPERATIONS

The activity of buying and selling government securities when it's done by the Federal Reserve System.

Open-market operations are set into motion at the monthly meeting of the Federal Open Market Committee (FOMC). At these gatherings, the governors of the Federal Reserve in Washington, along with the presidents of five regional Federal Reserve banks, vote on how to conduct monetary policy over the near term. Just what goes on at these meetings is a big secret until, weeks later, the minutes are published.

The operations themselves consist of the Fed buying or selling government securities. If, for example, the FOMC decides that the economy is growing too fast and inflation threatens, it takes securities from its own portfolio holdings and sells them on the open market.

The buyers pay for the securities by giving the Fed checks drawn on their banks. When the Fed presents those checks for payment, an interesting thing happens. The banks lose some of their "balances with the Fed," which means that their reserves are reduced. When bank reserves (assets) are reduced, the banks must, of course, reduce the amount of their deposits (liabilities). And since the banking system is a fractional reserve system in which reserves back only a fraction of loanable money, fewer reserves means a whole lot fewer deposits or bank-created money.

In other (fewer) words, the sale of government securities

reduces the amount of loan money available from banks, which means there is less credit in the system. Less credit, in turn, means higher interest rates. Higher interest rates, in turn, mean less business activity. Less business activity, in turn, means slower economic growth. And slower economic growth means, presumably, less inflation.

There is thus a rather long chain of events between the FOMC decision that the economy is overheating and the actual slowing of the economy. And in a big, complicated economy, a long chain of events leaves a lot of room for random mess-ups. Simply put, policy is one thing, results another. Nonetheless, open-market operations are considered to be the most powerful tool the Fed has in its management of monetary policy. That's why the small army of "Fed watchers" spends a lot of time guessing what will happen at FOMC meetings and then poring over the minutes when they're published. *See* BANKS AND BANKING; THE FED.

OPPORTUNITY COST

Theoretically, a measure of what could have been; practically, the amount of money given up to invest in one thing instead of investing in another.

At first blush, the concept of opportunity cost appears silly. Obviously when one invests $1,000 in stock A, one cannot then turn around and invest the same $1,000 in stock B. Nonetheless, if the act of giving up B in favor of A is not a matter of whim, then there must be some basis on which investors decide between the two alternatives. There is. It's called opportunity cost.

Take the earnings of a firm. Management can either pay it out to shareholders in the form of dividends or keep it to reinvest in the company. Presumably, management decides what to do by figuring out the opportunity cost of reinvesting the earnings. If the company can use the money for projects which will earn 10 percent while the best return its stockholders can earn investing in projects with similar risk is 8 percent, then management will be doing stockholders a financial favor by retaining the earnings. If not, of course, management should pay out the earnings in dividends so the shareholders can earn a higher return investing in other things.

OPTION

A contract between a buyer and seller which permits the holder to buy or sell something at a specific price during a specific period of time. That's the definition in standard English. The definition in standard financial jargon is even less penetrable. It runs something like this: a contract where the buyer pays a premium for the right, but not the obligation, to call away or put to the seller of the contract a specific amount of the underlying security at the exercise, or striking, price anytime before the option's expiration date.

Hold on. Granted, this sounds like one of those who-are-you-kidding definitions, and also granted, the vocabulary of financial options has more buzzwords than a sociology text. But the idea itself is not only fairly easy to understand but crucial for sophisticated financial players.

Take a simple option. In real estate, a potential buyer pays a fee which gives him or her the temporary right to buy a house at a specific price; he or she has an option to buy. In financial prose, that option is named a call option because the buyer has the right to "call away," or take away, something from the seller. (The opposite of a call option is a put option, which gives the buyer the right to sell something to the seller or, ungraciously, to "put it" to him.)

Take a less simple option. In the stock market, an investor who holds some actual shares in IBM can either pay a fee (premium) for the temporary right to sell those shares to another investor or collect a fee for granting the temporary right to have those shares purchased from him. In the first case, the investor has bought a put; in the second case, the investor has sold a call.

Now why would an investor want to go to all this trouble? To hedge his holding in IBM stock against loss.

Say that the market price for IBM is $200 a share. Buying put options with an exercise, or striking, price of $200 permits the investor to sell his shares for $200 even if the price of IBM falls to $150. In other words, he will be out the money he spent for the puts but will make money by exercising his right to sell the stock for a higher price. If, on the other hand, the price of IBM goes up, he will let his put options expire unexercised. In other words, he will be out the money he paid for the put options, but he will make money by selling the underlying, or actual, stock. Thus, he has hedged his position in IBM: If the price of the stock goes up, his total profit will be less than if he hadn't spent money buying put options; but if the price goes down, his total loss will be less because his puts allow him to make money by selling the stock at the higher exercise price.

Now say that the market price for IBM is $150. Selling call options at the exercise price of $150 allows the investor to make money (he pockets the premium) even if the price goes up to $200 and the buyer of the calls exercises her right to buy his stock for $150. Sure, he loses money when he loses the opportunity to sell his stock for $200, but that loss is cushioned by his sale of call options. In other words, if the price of the stock goes up, he misses out on some of the profit on the underlying stock, but he has made money on the options. If, on the other hand, the price goes down, the options he has sold will expire unexercised; he will have lost money on the stock (it has lost value) but will have made money by selling options.

There are, of course, two other possible positions, since there are both a buyer and a seller for every option contract. Thus, an investor could also buy calls or sell puts. If you think of a call option as an opportunity to buy and a put option as the opportunity to sell, then the investor can buy a buy or sell a sell . . .

Writing, or selling, calls is a classic strategy for investors who want to hedge their losses when their stocks decline in value. It is called covered option writing because they already own the actual stock; if the buyer of the calls exercises the right to call away their stock, these investors are "covered."

Investors who sell calls without owning the actual stock are said to be writing naked options; if the buyer of the calls exercises the right to call away the stock, the option seller is "naked" and must go into the market to purchase the stock. The purpose of writing naked options is not to hedge against loss in an actual stock but to make money speculating: If the price of the stock falls below the call options' exercise price, the options will expire unexercised and—voilà—the investor will have made money by selling something she didn't own.

And finally, here is one more dose of jargon. Exercise prices on options don't have to be identical to the market price of the stock on the day the options are bought or sold. For example, when the exercise price is well above the current market price of the stock, call options are said to be "out of the money," and when the exercise price is well below the current price, the options are said to be "in the money." (If the exercise price is close to the current price, then the options are "at the money.")

Individual stocks are not the only things on which options can be traded. There are also active options markets for stock indices, debt securities, foreign currencies, and futures contracts.

The alert will have noticed that this definition hasn't really said anything about the price of options. That's on purpose. Generally, options are a lot cheaper than an identical amount of actual stock, and in general the price of an option will depend on how much the exercise price or expiration date deviates from the current price or date. But what any one investor should pay for any one option depends on many considerations, some of which are known but can change from day to day, some of which are only approximately known, and some of which are unique to the investor. There are, however, lots of mathematical formulas which claim to take all these considerations into account, thereby yielding the correct price for buying or selling options. *See* HEDGING.

OVER-THE-COUNTER MARKET

The market for trading securities which are not listed on an organized stock exchange.

The OTC market is actually a giant network of dealers who use telephones and/or computers to execute trades. It is the largest market in the United States and covers everything from stocks of very small companies to U.S. government bonds. It is also what's called a negotiated market, meaning that many of the prices are—more or less—arrived at through—more or less—polite bickering. (Price information on OTC securities is quoted in two pieces: bid, the buyer's end, and ask, the seller's end.)

A sizable chunk of the OTC stock market comes under the purview of the National Association of Securities Dealers. The NASD both polices its members and runs the nationwide communications network known as NASDAQ, which has transformed this part of the OTC market into a slick, computerized trading system. Indeed, the NASD has been so successful in making the OTC market an efficient, world-class market that many companies which qualify for listing on the New York Stock Exchange—once the imprimatur of corporate success—now prefer to have their stock traded on NASDAQ. *See* NEW YORK STOCK EXCHANGE.

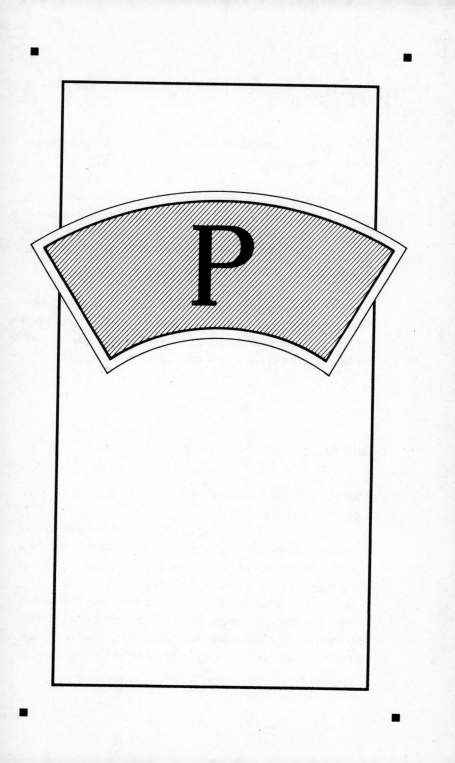

Partnership

Form of business organization in which two or more people share the risks and rewards.

There are two types of partnerships: a general partnership, in which each partner has unlimited liability or responsibility for the debts of the enterprise, including their personal assets; and a limited partnership, in which, by legal agreement, certain partners' liability extends only to the capital they've put into the enterprise, not to their personal assets.

Partnerships, which are found in professions like law, accounting, and medicine, are subject to a minimum of government regulation and taxation. That's good. What's bad is that if one of the partners dies or goes insane or bankrupt, the partnership either ends or gets tangled up in legal confusion.

Par Value

The nominal value printed on the face of a stock or bond, hence also called face value.

In the case of a preferred stock, dividend payments are usually made on the basis of par value; and in the case of a bond, interest payments are figured as a percentage of par and the principal payment at maturity is at par value.

Few securities actually trade at par; instead, they trade either above or below par. Take a $10,000 bond that carries 10 percent interest. If interest rates rise above 10 percent, the price, or real value, of the bond will fall below $10,000 to compensate investors for the bond's below-market rate of interest. If interest rates fall below 10 percent, the price of the bond will rise above $10,000. *See* FACE VALUE.

PENSION FUND

Money set aside by an employer to provide benefits, like a regular income, to employees after retirement.

The exact amount the employer sets aside, which is called a contribution, usually depends on how long the employee has worked at the company and how much he or she earns—the longer the service and the higher the salary, the larger the contribution.

There is no one way to run a pension fund. Some employers invest their pension money without consulting employees; others ask employees to allocate their pension money themselves to various investment funds like bond mutual funds or stock mutual funds. Some employers promise employees a specific amount on retirement—called a defined benefit plan—while others just promise to contribute a specific amount during employment—called a defined contribution plan. Some employers let employees make additional contributions from their wages; others do not.

Pension funds have become important financial players. Not only do they represent a large portion of individual savings, but by virtue of the megabillions of dollars that have been accumulated, they have come to represent a large portion of the institutional money which is invested in every aspect of the economy. *See* INSTITUTIONAL INVESTOR.

PONZI SCHEME

Clever business version of the chain letter in which investors are promised a quick, easy return on their money.

The Ponzi scheme was named after its inventor, Charles Ponzi, who perfected this seductive fraud in the 1920s. Seductive because not only is it simple, but it actually works. For a while. The cash flow depends on one set of investors being paid by another set of investors—usually the subsequent investors are brought in by the initial investors. In other words, returns are paid to investors with cash from a fresh set of investors . . . and so on and so forth.

Typically, the Ponzi mastermind offers the first round of investors a fabulous return, or interest payment, on their money in a very short time; he bases that offer on a fabulous investment opportunity that he alone has discovered. During that period, the Ponzi mastermind gathers similar payments from the second round of investors, which then enables him to pay the first set their "fabulous return." The Ponzi mastermind then offers to return the original stake to the first investors. Usually, however, that round is hooked on making such easy money, and they stay in for another round. Ditto for the subsequent investors. The round robin comes to an end when the Ponzi mastermind either disappears with the money or announces that the fabulous investment has flopped and the money is gone.

A variation on the classic Ponzi scheme is called a pyramid scheme because each round requires an increase in the number of investors, so the arrangement comes to resemble a pyramid. Consider:

Typically, a promoter offers investors the right to sell distributorships (which may or may not actually sell products to the public) in return for an initial investment; investors must also rebate to the promoter some of the money they make from selling distributorships.

So. Say the promoter sells distributorships to Chump and Schlump for $5,000 apiece with the agreement that they will rebate half of their profits from selling distributorships. That means that the promoter rakes in $10,000 from the initial sale and another $10,000 when Chump and Schlump sell two distributorships each, which they must do to break even on their original investment. If Chump and Schlump want to make a profit, they must sell at least three distributorships each (which, of course, nets the promoter another $5,000).

So far, so good. But each of the six investors that Chump and Schlump found must also sell two distributorships each to break even, three to make a profit. That makes eighteen total. And each of those eighteen must sell three apiece, which makes fifty-four. And so it goes until there is literally nobody left to sell distributorships to. Of course, as long as Chump and Schlump are near the top of pyramid, they will make money.

There are lots of variations on the Ponzi scheme, and each and every one is considered a fraud by the legal authorities. Ponzi masterminds and promoters who are caught face jail; those who are not caught will make a ton of money; and most investors—whether the Ponzi mastermind is caught or not— will lose their money.

PORTFOLIO

Specifically defined—a collection of the securities held by an investor. Generally defined—a collection of the assets held by an investor. The former, for example, would not include houses (or, more properly put, real estate holdings).

Whether the value of your portfolio is comfortingly large or cringingly small, there is one principle that most financial types espouse. You should have what is called a well-diversified portfolio. Why? To reduce the risk that the value of your portfolio will fall with the misfortunes of one, or a few, bad investments. (Of course, that also means you reduce the chances that the value of your portfolio will skyrocket with the fortunes of one, or a few, dynamite investments.)

Well-diversified usually means a portfolio that includes a lot of different assets like stocks, bonds, gold, or even art and precious gems. That way, if flaming inflation erodes the value of your stocks and bonds, the total worth of your portfolio will remain relatively constant because the same flaming inflation will swell the value of your gold and diamonds.

Some people give their portfolios to professionals to manage, either because they don't have the time, energy, or interest to do it themselves or because their own track record indicates that they don't have the timing, instinct, or good sense to do it successfully. Whatever. There is now a whole army of Wall Streeters, from big institutions to small boutiques, which manage other people's portfolios.

PREFERRED STOCK

A security which resembles a bond more than it does a common stock. (If you think that definition is not exactly illuminating, you're right; but when you read the rest of this entry, you'll see more light.)

Preferred stock is like a bond because it carries a par value on which its payments—called dividends—are determined and fixed, much like interest payments on bonds. (Thus, just like bonds, the market price of preferred stock varies, but the dollar amount of its payments does not. Too, like bonds, preferred stock can be issued as securities which are convertible into common stock.)

Preferred stock is, however, unlike a bond because the issuing corporation can omit the dividend without having to go bankrupt. Also, preferred stock is unlike a bond because it doesn't carry a maturity date. (Although some preferred stock is callable, which can limit its life.)

Two additional things just to confuse matters more: Preferred stock is less risky than common stock because corporations cannot pay dividends to common stock holders until preferred holders have been paid all the dividends to which they are entitled. And in the event of bankruptcy, the claims of the preferred stock holders on the assets of the company come before the claims of common stock holders—but after the bondholders. *See* CONVERTIBLE.

PRICE-EARNINGS RATIO

The market price of a stock divided by its earnings per share.

The P/E is one of the traditional measures investors use to decide whether a stock is a good buy or a bad one because it is taken as an indication of how fast the company's earnings will grow: The higher the P/E, the faster the potential growth in earnings.

Using P/Es involves a lot of first-rate Wall Street lingo. The P/E is actually a multiple: If the price of the stock is $100 and its earnings are $5 per share, then its multiple is twenty. (Ergo, the stock is selling at twenty times its earnings power.)

The stock's multiple is usually compared to the multiple of the stock market as a whole. If the market multiple is fifteen and the stock's multiple is twenty, then some potential investors will say, "Whoa, that stock is overvalued, investors are paying too much for it." Still others will say, "Wow, that stock must have great growth prospects, otherwise investors wouldn't be willing to pay $100 a share." In other words, like most financial measures, the meaning of P/E is somewhat subjective. *See* FINANCIAL RATIOS.

PRIME RATE

The rate of interest on loans that is charged by banks to their best customers, usually large corporations with the best credit rating.

Since the prime rate reflects a bank's highest confidence level that its loan will be repaid, it usually represents the lowest interest rate available. It also serves as the basis on which other interest rates—like mortgage rates—are determined. When banks change their prime rates, other interest rates change accordingly; thus it's big news when banks move the prime up or down. (The plural is intentional; when one bank changes its prime, you can be sure that almost all others will follow in a day or two.) *See* INTEREST.

Profits

Whatever, if anything, is left over after a business has paid all its bills; more formally, profits equal revenues minus expenses. Also called net income.

There are, of course, all sorts of ways to look at profits. There is, for example, gross profit, which is the difference between sales and the cost of goods sold. There is something called profit margin, which is the ratio of net profit to sales. (This measure is used to determine how efficient a company is compared to the industry, or to compare different industries with each other.)

Presumably, different profit measures are useful to different groups—accountants focus on one, stock analysts on another, investors on something else, and company management on yet another thing entirely. Baldly put, profit is a rather spongy word —one person's giant profit may be another person's meager showing.

Pro forma

A hypothetical statement.

Companies use pro formas when engaging in what is called financial planning. Typically, constructing a pro forma involves assuming that something will happen in the future, like a fabulous increase in sales, and then figuring out what future financial statements would look like under that assumption. This exercise supposedly tells the company what to expect if its projections are realized—whether its wildest dreams will come true or whether it ought to go back to the drawing board.

Program trading

(And just to get the MEGO [my eyes glaze over] factor out of the way—often called stock index futures arbitrage.) Market strategy using computers programmed to buy or sell vast amounts of securities, usually to take advantage of very small price discrepancies.

Program trading is a gift of the high-tech age. Typically, it involves a computer program that evaluates the differences that can develop between the prices of actual stocks and the prices of futures contracts on a stock index made up of those stocks.

Huh? Hold on, here's an example. When the price of the futures contract on the Standard & Poor's Index of 500 stocks rises above the prices of the actual stocks, it may make sense to arbitrage—to sell the futures (the expensive securities) and buy the actual stocks (the cheap securities). *May* make sense.

It makes sense only if the return from this arbitrage is above an alternative return, like the yield on three-month Treasury notes; again, this is something that the computer figures out.

This is one form of program trading. Others involve stock indexes and the futures; still others are triggered by complicated strategies—called portfolio insurance—designed to limit losses in falling markets.

The intricacies of program trading strategies may be difficult for a rookie to master at first pass, but their effect on the market is not. When computers at big brokerage houses, investment banks, and institutional investors all flash a buy-the-actual-stocks signal, these megaplayers slurp up stocks, sending the market up like a rocket. If, on the other hand, the computers all flash a sell-the-stocks signal, the mass dumping of stocks drops the market like a stone. And all this activity can literally take place in a few minutes.

There's no question that program trading can upset the markets. And no question that it has, in turn, upset many investors and observers. But none of this means there is anything wrong with the practice. On the contrary: Many of these same instruments are used for hedging risk, and the activity of arbitraging —buying cheap and simultaneously selling dear—brings the prices in all markets into line. Too, the markets themselves usually return to their preprogram levels in a matter of days following the upset.

PROPRIETORSHIP

A type of business organization in which one person owns the business—he or she alone enjoys the rewards and suffers the risks.

Proprietorships, which are common in farming and retailing, are simple to start and not subject to much government regulation. That's good. What's bad is that the owner has unlimited liability for the debts of the enterprise, including his or her personal assets.

PROXY

A document which gives one person the authority to act for another.

Most investors encounter a proxy when it is sent to them by a company in which they hold stock. By signing the proxy, the shareholder gives the company's management the right to vote his or her shares on questions of policy or elections to the board of directors. This has led some to suggest that shareholders get what they deserve when management goes ahead and makes foolish decisions or packs the board with a bunch of rubber stamps.

PUT

See OPTION.

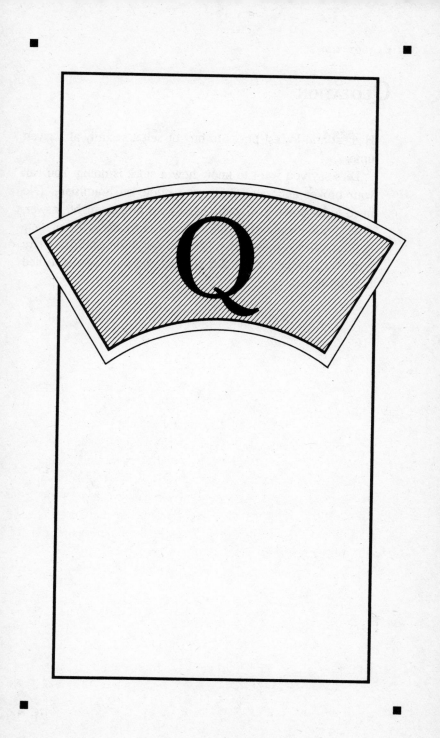

QUOTATION

Highest and lowest prices to buy or sell a security at a given time.

Let's say you want to know how a stock is doing. You call your broker and say, "Give me a quote on Framistan." (No need to be polite to your broker.) Your broker might answer, "The bid is twenty-five and a quarter, the offer is twenty-five and a half." He means that you can sell it for $25.25 a share and you can buy it for $25.50. Bid-and-offer is also called bid-and-asked.

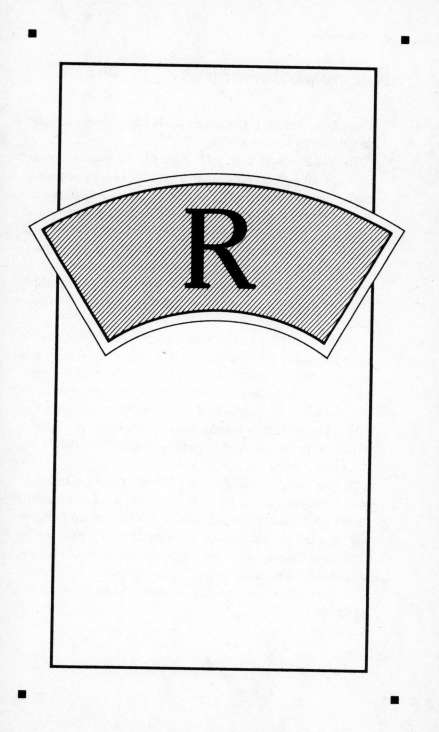

RANDOM WALK HYPOTHESIS

Theory about stock prices which holds that nobody can really outwit the stock market.

The random walk theory fits right into the efficient market theory. That is, if the stock market is efficient—all new information is immediately reflected in stock prices—then changes in stock prices are random. How so? Because bad news and good news happen with equal frequency, so both positive and negative price changes based on new information also happen with equal frequency. And if price changes are just as likely to be negative as positive, then it's impossible to predict which direction those changes will take. Price changes are thus random.

If the random walk hypothesis is correct, then it's impossible to predict future prices on the basis of past prices. A stock that has gone down is just as likely to go up—or to go down some more. Too, it is unlikely that any investor can consistently outperform the market by picking "undervalued" stocks. Investors may get lucky with their picks, but over the long term, individual stock prices are likely to rise or fall no faster than the market as a whole.

All this suggests a strategy of randomly picking a bunch of stocks and just holding them. In fact, every so often a puckish investor will start something akin to the Dart Board Fund, in which stocks are selected by throwing darts at a page in *The Wall Street Journal*. A more sophisticated and less amusing strategy would be to buy into an index fund which is especially designed to track the market. *See* EFFICIENT MARKET HYPOTHESIS; INDEX FUND.

REAL ESTATE INVESTMENT TRUST

Vehicle which allows people to buy shares in a portfolio of real estate assets.

A REIT is like a closed-end fund or an investment company. The number of shares in the trust is fixed, the portfolio itself is managed by a group of professionals, and the stocks of some REITs trade on stock exchanges. REITs are offered by a variety of institutions: insurance companies, brokerage houses, banks, and mortgage houses.

The real estate assets held by the trust can take two forms: mortgages or loans which use real estate as collateral, or actual real estate properties. (In the latter case, the trust serves as the landlord.)

The allure for investors is the ability to double-diversify their assets—once by diversifying into real estate and again by diversifying the real estate into more than one holding. The income from the trust is passed through to the investors.

REGISTRATION STATEMENT

Statement of facts which must be filed with the Securities and Exchange Commission before a company can issue new securities to the public. *See* SECURITIES AND EXCHANGE COMMISSION.

REVENUE BOND

See MUNICIPAL BOND.

RISK

The chance, or probability, that a decision will result in an unpleasant or pleasant outcome.

So what else is new? Life, after all, is risky. What's new—or at least different—is that it is possible to quantify the risk involved in financial or investment decisions. To give a specific example, the riskiness of an individual stock is thought to be captured by its beta: The higher the beta number, the more risky the stock. Thus, a person who is risk averse can use betas to get an idea of which stocks would cause him sleepless nights.

Indeed, there are people who would never consider calculating the odds of getting hit by a truck when they venture out but who wouldn't even think of venturing their money without, at the very least, constructing a probability tree—an exercise which entails listing the possible outcomes of an investment decision, from enormous profits to zippo, and attaches numbers to the likelihood of each of those outcomes.

Investors can use these numbers games to figure out how much profit (return) an investment might yield and whether the return would be large enough to compensate for the risk. Thus, a risk-averse person might be willing to take on more risk if he figures the return will be high. This is known as the trade-off between risk and return.

It all sounds marvelously simple and straightforward, and in some cases it is. In other cases, the numbers exercise is unbelievably muddled, and the probabilities assigned to the outcomes are just guesses.

At any rate, the possibility of quantifying risk should not beg the question of what makes one investment riskier than another. Lots of things affect risk. Consider, for example, the nature of the investment. Obviously, buying a U.S. Treasury bond is less risky than breaking ground for a computer chip factory. Too, there are the properties of the investment itself. A U.S. Treasury bond is not entirely without the risk that interest rates will rise above the bond's rate. So, too, the general economic climate contributes to risk. In this case, interest rate risk is affected by the rate of inflation, which is, in turn, affected by other factors. And so it goes. *See* BETA COEFFICIENT; HEDGING; LIQUIDITY.

Rollover

For a borrower, the process of renewing a loan by extending its term; for the lender, the process of investing the proceeds of one security in another, new security.

While anyone can roll over debt, it reaches its highest form in the refunding practices of the U.S. Treasury. Here, the Treasury replaces its maturing debt with new issues of debt rather than paying off the maturing debt with cash.

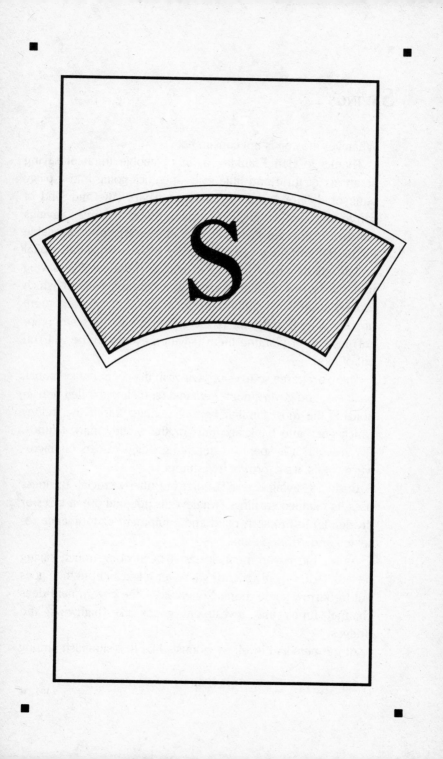

SAVINGS

Whatever income is not consumed.

Thanks to Ben Franklin, a lot of people think of saving as an act of thrift and little else—pennies going into a piggy bank or dollars under the mattress. That's cute and kind of comforting, but savings are much more dynamic. Savings which are not shoved under a mattress are funds available for investment; they can be used to replace worn-out capital and to create new forms of capital. In other words, saving underwrites the capital stock of the country, without which economic growth would come to a halt. Put another, more homely way, if a farmer (society) consumes his seeds (capital) instead of planting them (saving), eventually he will run out of food.

There are three sources of savings in the economy: personal, business, and government. Personal (sometimes called household) is the most familiar type of savings; this is the money which goes into bank accounts or the money market funds. (Even when it is spent on durable goods, like cars or microwave ovens, it's a form of investment.)

Business saving is less familiar but utterly crucial. Business uses its retained earnings (whatever is not paid out in taxes or dividends) to invest in plant and equipment or to finance research and development.

As for the government, it hasn't been doing much saving recently—it not only spends whatever it takes in but then goes out to borrow some more. Nonetheless, the government does channel funds into investment goods like highways and bridges.

At the personal level, economists like to distinguish among

different motives for saving. For instance, people can save for retirement or against unexpected events.

As for the exact proportion of income saved, that can be a function of several things. Generally, people with higher incomes save more. (Common sense: Poorer people must spend a higher proportion of their income just to house, clothe, and feed themselves.) The amount saved can also depend on inflation; the higher the rate, the less incentive to save, since inflation erodes the value of savings. It can also depend on the return to saving; higher interest rates make saving more attractive. Tax policy can also increase the incentive to save by increasing the after-tax return on saving. And finally, people who feel that their future prospects are solid will save less than those who are afraid, for example, of losing their job.

There are countless ways to save—or, to use a slogan, to make your money work for you. People can invest in the stock market, in bank certificates of deposit, or in U.S. bonds. They can salt money away in an Individual Retirement Account or in a life insurance policy. In fact, there are even some ways of saving over which people have little control. The federal government "forces" people to save via the Social Security payroll tax, and some employers set aside a portion of wages and salaries in private pension programs.

SECURITIES

Strictly speaking, things that are pledged as collateral to back up a loan. Less strictly, documents that represent claims on income or wealth such as stocks and bonds. (The fancy term for bonds, for example, is fixed income securities.)

SECURITIES AND EXCHANGE COMMISSION

Federal regulatory agency established in 1934 to police U.S. securities laws.

The main job of the SEC is to protect the investing public from being fleeced by the investment community, that army of people found in brokerage houses, investment banks, stock exchanges, public corporations, and other less savory places and who have been known to engage in insider trading, the manipulation of stock prices, and various other kinds of fraud.

The SEC is supposed to make sure that the laws against these activities are obeyed. The most visible mechanism of this enforcement is reams and reams of paperwork. For example, when corporations issue securities, they are required to file registration statements with the SEC making "full disclosure" of the character of the security; they must also regularly file detailed financial information, called a 10-K.

SHORT

The practice of selling a security that is not owned by the seller in the hope that its price will fall.

Simple, really. Say that Framistan's stock is selling at $10. And say that you think the market price is too high and that investors are bound to recognize this and sell their shares, which will bring down the price. Say you don't own any Framistan stock and you surely don't want to buy it if the price is about to fall. What do you do?

Well, you could borrow 100 shares from a brokerage house and sell them at the market price. You would pocket the $1,000 from the sale, but you would also owe the brokerage house 100 shares of Framistan. But if your prediction is correct and Framistan's price falls to $5, you could go into the market and buy 100 shares for $500. You could then return the shares to the brokerage house, thus clearing the books (called closing out your position) and a $500 profit. If, however, your assessment is wrong and Framistan's price rises to $15, you would be in the lamentable position of having to replace the borrowed stock at a cost of $1,500—$500 more than the price for which you sold it. You would then be out $500.

Short selling is just another nifty way to make money playing the market. That is, just as investors want to buy low and sell high in a rising market, short selling offers them the opportunity to sell high and buy low in a falling market. Short selling is also practiced by investors who want to hedge risk. *See* BEAR; HEDGING; LONG.

SINKING FUND

Place in which money to pay off a debt accumulates.

Usually the debtor, a firm or local government, plunks some money into the sinking fund each year so that the necessary funds are on hand when the time to pay off the debt arrives or when the time to retire the debt seems right. Thus, a debt that is covered by a sinking fund is considered to be less risky than one that isn't.

SPECULATION

Buying or selling something in the hope that a profit can be made from a favorable price change.

The alert might wonder if that definition is a little too general; after all, it makes the act of speculation sound a lot like the act of investing. Well, the two *are* alike, despite the fact that most people take great pains to distinguish them.

On one end of the spectrum, there is the moral distinction —speculating is bad, investing is good; on the other end, there is the technical distinction—speculating involves taking on more risk than does investing. Thus the term "speculation" is used to describe anything done by shady types in wild and exotic markets, as in "a currency speculator." And investment is used to describe anything done by upright citizens in staid and familiar markets, as in "an art investor."

These distinctions are silly. A person can speculate in art or invest in currencies. Both are done with an eye to financial gain—the work of art might be sold later for profit and the currency could appreciate, giving it more buying power. Both entail varying degrees of risk, depending on the specific situation—buying the work of an unknown artist, for example, is probably riskier than buying francs for a summer vacation in France. *See* INVESTMENT.

SPOT MARKET

Market in which commodities are sold for cash and delivered, well, on the spot.

The spot market and the futures market are very closely linked. For example, the prices in both markets tend to fluctuate together since the prices in both respond to fundamentals like the supply-and-demand situation for the particular commodity. (A drought in the corn belt would tend to drive up both the spot and futures prices of corn.)

Nonetheless, there are important differences between the two markets. Deals struck in the spot market are negotiated (I'll sell you so many bushels for so much money), and delivery is immediate (where would you like your purchases delivered?). Contracts in the futures market are standardized and are usually closed out before delivery time.

The spot market is also known as the cash market, and the spot price is also known as the cash price. *See* COMMODITY; FUTURES MARKET.

SPREAD

The difference between the price a buyer is willing to pay for a security (the bid) and the price a seller is willing to sell (the asked). Generally, the less liquid the security, the larger the spread.

STANDARD & POOR'S 500 COMPOSITE INDEX

Index of the market value of the share prices of 425 industrial companies, fifty utilities, and twenty-five railroads.

The S&P is computed by the Standard & Poor's Corporation. Since the S&P is a much broader index of the stock market than the Dow-Jones Industrial Average—and thus a better measure of market performance—it is more popular among professional money managers. When these pros talk about whether the market is up or down, they refer to the S&P; when amateurs, including the media, talk about the market, they refer to the DJ. *See* DOW-JONES AVERAGES.

STOCK DIVIDEND, STOCK SPLIT

The first is issuance to shareholders of additional new shares of stock instead of a cash payment. The second is the issuance to shareholders of new shares of stock. A three-for-one split, for example, would give each shareholder three new shares for each old share.

The effect of either maneuver is the same: Issuing more shares without much else having changed means that the price of each share will fall because supply has increased without demand increasing as well. *See* EX-DIVIDEND.

STOCK EXCHANGE

An organized marketplace in which securities are bought and sold and where the buyers and sellers come together in—more or less—one place.

There are seven stock exchanges in the United States. The big mother is the New York Stock Exchange. The others are the American Stock Exchange (a smaller version of the NYSE) and five regional exchanges (Pacific, Cincinnati, Boston, Midwest, and Philadelphia—much, much smaller versions of the NYSE). The regional exchanges give local companies which are too small or too peculiar to merit listing on the big mother a chance to have their stock traded on an organized exchange.

There's a long-running debate over whether the physical marketplace afforded by a stock exchange is necessary, given the technological achievements of the electronic marketplace afforded by the NASDAQ over-the-counter system. At present, opinion seems to favor trading by electronic blip over human outcry. *See* AMERICAN STOCK EXCHANGE; NEW YORK STOCK EXCHANGE; OVER-THE-COUNTER MARKET.

STOP ORDER

Order to a broker to buy or sell something if the market price rises or falls by a certain amount.

Whaa? Okay: Usually a stop order is designed to limit losses or protect gains on a position already held. If, for instance, you are long a stock, then your stop order might be to sell if the price falls by a certain amount; and if you are short a stock, then your stop order might be to buy (or cover your short position) if the price rises by a certain amount. *See* LIMIT ORDER; MARKET ORDER.

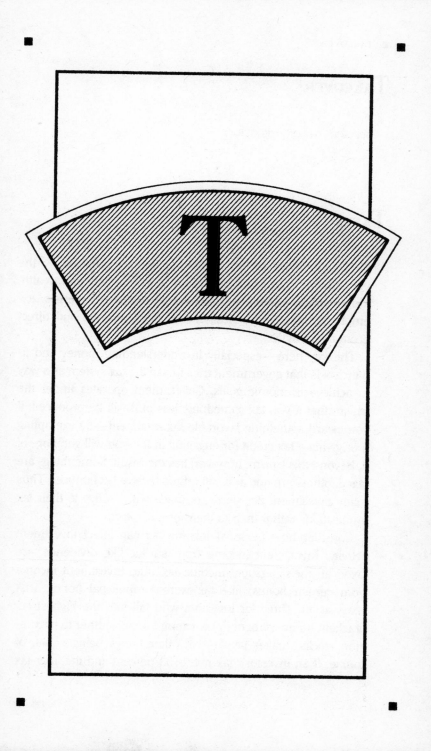

■ TAKEOVER

TAKEOVER

See ACQUISITION; MERGER.

TAXES

Simple, if rather lifeless, definition: money collected by the government from levies on income, consumption, and wealth. More realistic definition: complicated system of charges, exemptions, and credits designed to raise revenue and direct economic activity.

The key here—especially in understanding money and finance—is that government tries to use the tax system as a way to achieve economic goals. Government operates under the truism that if you tax something, less of it will be produced; if you award something favorable tax treatment—by exempting it or giving a tax credit for engaging in it—you will get more of it. Beyond this truism, however, lies the result: Some things are taxed, others are not, and still others receive tax bonuses. Thus many investment decisions are made with an eye to their tax implications rather than to their intrinsic worth.

Consider how personal income tax can affect investment activity. Investment income from stocks, like dividends, are taxed at one's personal income tax rate. Investment income from certain bonds, like tax-exempt municipal bonds, isn't taxed at all. Thus, for investors who fall into the highest tax brackets, an investment in tax-exempt bonds, rather than common stocks, makes sense. (All other things being equal, of course. If an investor's tax rate is 33 percent and the after-tax rate on taxable investments is around 10 percent, then the return on tax-exempts ought to be about 7 percent.)

Ditto for corporate income tax. When firms raise capital by borrowing it—say, by issuing bonds—the interest payments are tax-deductible; when they raise capital by issuing new stock, they do not get a tax deduction from their income. Thus, tax policy creates a strong incentive for firms to raise money by borrowing, as well as a strong incentive for potential investors to consider a firm's tax position along with more familiar considerations.

These examples are just the tip of the iceberg. The tax code is literally littered with inducements, discouragements, and loopholes which in turn distort investment decisions so that capital is not always directed to projects which offer the highest (pretax) rates of return. Too, the frustration generated by such a tax system can cause outright tax evasion—either by cheating, like failing to file a return, or by seeking out tax havens, like becoming a citizen of Luxembourg or Monaco.

TAX-EXEMPT

See MUNICIPAL BOND.

TENDER OFFER

A bid by either outsiders or management to purchase a firm's securities.

A tender offer made to current shareholders by outsiders is usually part of a hostile takeover. The outsiders offer shareholders a (usually) substantial premium over the average market price of the stock. That forces management into one of three positions: making a matching tender offer to the shareholders, making a tender offer to the outsiders (also called paying greenmail), or asking the shareholders to refuse the outsiders' tender offer and let them continue to manage.

None of these have totally terrific results. In the first two cases, management's tender offer draws down the firm's resources, and in the third case, it is a matter of time (if at all) before management can successfully manage the firm so that share prices rise to the level of the initial tender offer. *See* ACQUISITION; MERGER.

TIGHT MONEY

An apt phrase for an involved idea. "Tight" refers to the monetary policy undertaken by the Federal Reserve and "money" refers to the amount of money in the economy.

When the Fed decides to restrict the availability of credit in the economy, it clamps down on the supply of money. This causes interest rates to rise and borrowing to become unattractive. In other words, tight money means that the Fed has reined in the growth of money.

The opposite of tight money is loose money. *See* THE FED; LOOSE MONEY.

Treasury Securities

Debt obligations (IOUs) issued by the U.S. government.

Treasury bills: The shortest-term security. T-bills come in four maturities: ninety-one days, six months, nine months, and one year. They usually come in face values of $10,000.

Treasury notes: The intermediate-term security—anything over one year but less than ten. T-notes come in face values of $1,000 and up and have snazzy coupons entitling the owner to semiannual interest payments.

Treasury bonds: The longest-term security—anything over ten years. T-bonds come in face values of $1,000 and up and have snazzy coupons entitling the owner to semiannual interest payments.

Since Treasuries are an obligation of the U.S. government, they carry a very low risk of default. There is also an extremely active secondary market for them, so there's very little liquidity risk. The longer their terms, however, the more subject they are to the risk that either interest rates or inflation will rise, thus eroding their value. In short, Treasuries are kind of like a super form of cash—although they carry the same risks as cash, they also offer interest payments.

Treasury Stock

Common stock issued by a corporation and then reacquired by it.

TRUST

Money or property which is administered by somebody for the benefit (presumably) of somebody else.

Trusts are little triangles: They are set up by the point with the money or property (grantor), so that a second point (trustee) can control the money or property (fund), in order to provide for the third point (beneficiary). A trust can be set up when the grantor is alive but doesn't want to be bothered with managing the fund or for when the grantor dies and can't be bothered with managing, or when the beneficiary is a minor, incompetent, or otherwise irresponsible. Charities and estates are often set up as trusts.

Grantors may specify the investment and disbursement policies of the trust or just trust (sorry) the laws of whatever state the trust is established in. Grantors may also name a specific trustee, although generally trusts are administered by trust departments of trust companies or banks.

A trust is a legal arrangement. Thus, if the beneficiaries are unhappy with the trustee's management—which is often the case—it's tough for them to "break" the trust and get at the assets.

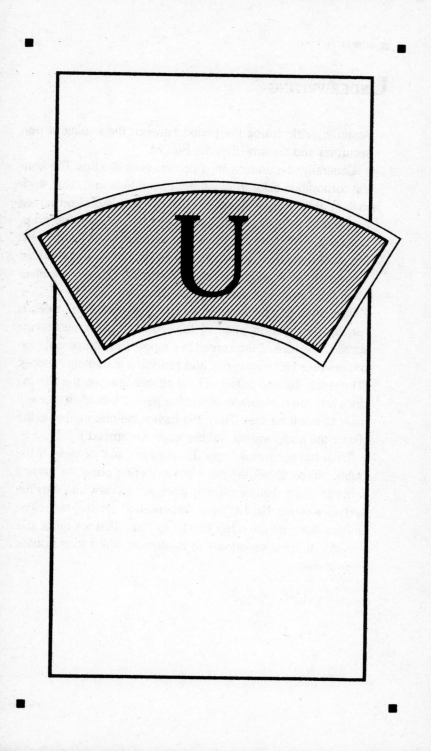

UNDERWRITING

Assuming risk during the period between the issuing of new securities and the time they are bought.

Generally, the underwriting process goes like this: The issuing corporation asks an investment bank to help it issue stock to the public. Help includes all sorts of things, like determining how much of the security should be issued and at what price. But most important, it means that the underwriter purchases the stock and then sells it to the public. Often the anointed investment bank will put together an underwriting syndicate of other firms to help it with the purchasing and selling.

The price at which the underwriter purchases the stock is usually the offering price of the stock minus a percentage spread. The size of the spread is supposed to compensate the underwriter for bearing risk and providing marketing services. (The risk is that the public will not be willing to pay the offering price and the underwriter will either get stuck holding it or will have to sell it for less. Thus, the higher the offering price, the riskier the underwriting and the larger the spread.)

What happens next depends on one's point of view. If the public slurps up all the stock at its offering price, the issuing firm can claim that the offering price was too low and thus the spread was too big (it "overcompensated" for the risk). The underwriters, on the other hand, can claim that the quick sale was due to their superiority in marketing, which thus justifies their spread.

Unlisted security

Security that is traded in the over-the-counter market and thus not listed on a stock exchange. *See* LISTED SECURITY.

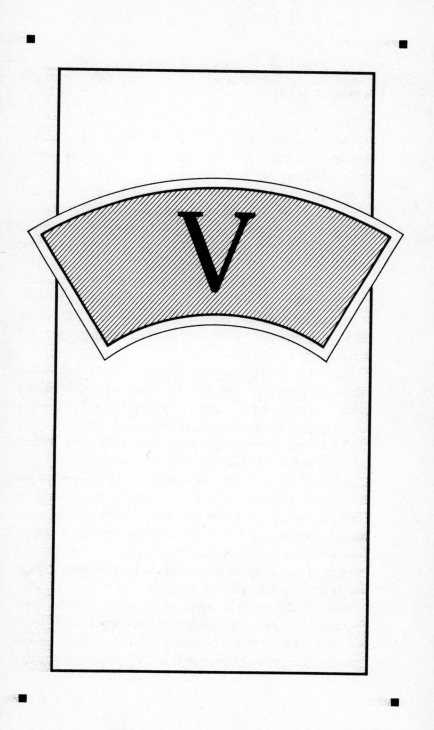

VARIABLE RATE

Instrument where either the rate of interest or the return on investment is free to fluctuate with other interest rates or with the performance of the underlying assets.

Example one: *Variable rate annuity.* An insurance contract which guarantees the annuitant an income based on the performance of the stocks held in the insurer's portfolio. (If the stocks do really well, the income will be really juicy—and vice versa.)

Example two: *Variable rate life insurance.* A contract in which death benefits are based on the performance of the stocks held in the insurer's portfolio. (Same as above: If the stocks are all dogs, then the death benefits will be disappointing—and vice versa.)

Example three: *Variable rate mortgage.* A mortgage contract where the interest charges are free to vary with other interest rates. Usually, however, there are a ceiling and a floor that put a limit on how much the mortgage rates can vary.

Variable rates were an invention of uncertain times. When rates on long-term contracts were fixed, significant and sustained increases in the rate of inflation—as happened in the 1970s—left lenders holding the bag. (For example, lenders, like mortgage banks, found that they were paying more for their new funds than they were earning on their old mortgage contracts. The holders of those mortgages with low rates of interest, of course, found themselves in the happy situation of paying below-market interest charges.)

Variable rates are more than a hedge against inflation. They also spread the risk more evenly between borrowers and lenders. In variable rate annuities, for example, the annuitants (lenders) bear some of the risk that the insurers (borrowers) will not be able to earn good investment returns. Under fixed rate annuities, if insurers didn't earn enough to pay the agreed-on return, they had to make up the difference from other funds.

Venture capital

"Venture" refers to a high-risk business or activity; "capital" refers to the money used to fund the venture.

Generally, the term has come to mean financing for small, start-up businesses which can't get financing from traditional sources. The suppliers of venture capital often take a big equity position in the company with the understanding that their pay-off will be many years away—if at all. Remember, these are high-risk enterprises. Of course, if all goes well, the return on venture capital can be terrifically high.

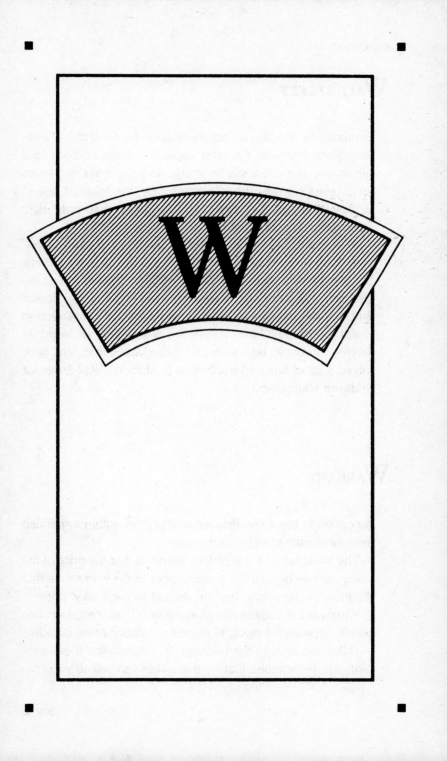

WALL STREET

Symbolically, the all-purpose designation for American capitalism. Metaphorically, the term applied to most anybody in a pin-striped suit and a silk tie who looks prosperous and wears an expensive wristwatch. Geographically, the financial district in lower Manhattan. Precisely, the street that runs right through the financial district.

In the old days, the geographic designation "Wall Street" really did mean the location of most of the important players: big banks, insurance companies, brokerage houses, stock exchanges, you name it. Nowadays, however, financial capital and activity are spread not only across the country (you've heard of Chicago) but across the world (you've heard of Tokyo). Moreover, high rents and limited space to expand have forced a lot of financial institutions to abandon Wall Street for midtown Manhattan.

WARRANT

An option to buy a specified amount of stock within a specified amount of time at a specified price.

The attraction of a warrant, of course, is that the price of the stock will rise beyond the exercise price of the warrant, so that the lucky owner gets to buy the stock at below market price.

Warrants are usually issued along with other securities, like bonds or preferred stock, to make the offering more attractive —called sweetening the package. In some cases, these warrants are detachable; that is, the owner can sell them separately from the securities. (Warrants trade on the major stock exchanges and in the over-the-counter market.) Warrants can also be issued to shareholders instead of cash or stock dividends.

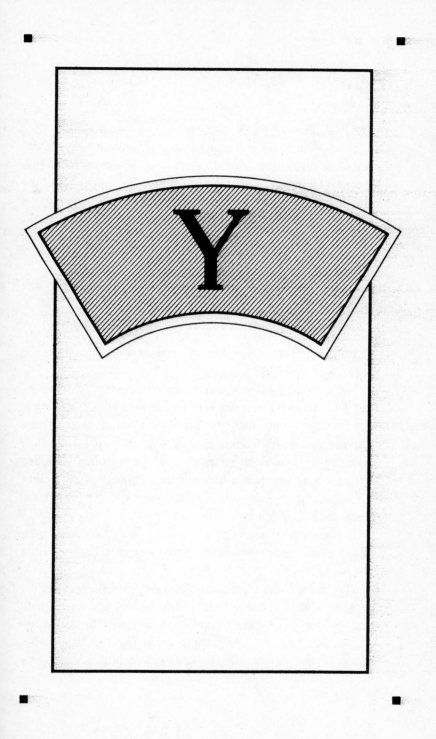

YIELD

The rate of return on an investment.

Yields, which are expressed in percentages, are easy to figure. Just divide the annual return from the investment (the income) by the amount of the investment (the price). Thus, the yield from a $10,000 investment in the stock of a company that pays an annual dividend of $500 is 5 percent. *See* BOND YIELD.

YIELD CURVE

Relationship between yields and maturities of fixed income securities as plotted on a graph.

Consider a typical yield curve, like the one for U.S. Treasuries. The range of yields appears on the vertical axis, starting at the point of origin with the lowest; the range of maturities appears on the horizontal axis, starting at the point of origin with the shortest. Each security's yield and maturity is plotted with a point, and then a line is drawn through all the points. The resulting line, or curve, can be upward-sloping from left to right, flattish, or downward-sloping.

Plotting a yield curve for a bond is a snap; interpreting the shape of that curve, however, is what separates the men from the boys.

The shape of the yield curve illustrates something called the term structure of interest rates. If the curve slopes up (as it usually does), it's because rates on longer-term bonds are higher than rates on shorter-term ones. That can happen because of one or two things—although it probably happens because of both and the explanation always sounds a little less than precise. If bond buyers expect interest and inflation rates to go up in the future, then they will demand higher rates (or lower prices) on longer-term bonds; if bond buyers prefer shorter holding periods because they want to stay relatively liquid, then they will accept lower rates (or higher prices) on shorter-term bonds.

At any rate (small joke), when the yield curve slopes up, it is thought to be a sign that investors expect interest and inflation rates to go up; when the yield curve slopes down, it is thought to be a sign that investors expect interest and inflation rates to go down. *See* BOND YIELD.

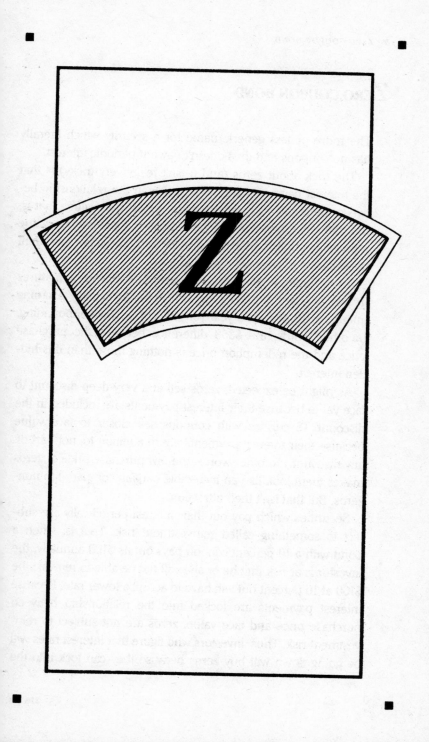

ZERO COUPON BOND

The more or less generic name for a security which literally has no coupons and thus doesn't pay out periodic interest.

The trick about zeros (and it isn't really very tricky) is that the interest payments are hidden away in the relationship between the security's purchase price and its face value. That is, the difference between the zero's cost and redemption value represents implicit interest—interest earned but not paid until the security reaches full maturity.

An example: A zero which is worth $1,000 when it matures in twenty years and sells for $142 today is actually accruing interest at 10 percent a year (on the $142) plus compounding. In other words, the $858 difference between the purchase price and the redemption price is nothing more than this hidden interest.

As might be expected, zeros sell at a very deep discount to face value because their interest payments are included in the discount. (Securities with coupons sell closer to face value because their interest payments are in addition to, not part of, any discount.) In other words, the low purchase price of zeros makes them look like an incredible bargain compared to non-zeros. But that isn't their attraction.

Securities which pay out their interest periodically are subject to something called reinvestment risk. That is, when a bond with a 10 percent coupon pays out its $100 annually, the investor is at risk that he or she will not be able to reinvest the $100 at 10 percent but will have to accept a lower rate. Because interest payments are locked into the relationship between purchase price and face value, zeros are not subject to reinvestment risk. Thus, investors who figure that interest rates will be going down will buy zeros because they can lock into the higher rate. (Of course, if these investors guess wrong and interest rates go up, then they would have been better off investing in a security with periodic payouts of interest.) *See* BOND; BOND YIELD.